This new book on the creeds of t welcome, for in a relatively sma historical context, the theological impor, and the of the affirmations of these time-honoured and normative texts. And it does all of this in language that is easy to grasp, which is no small feat, for often experts on these creeds are hard put to explain them in comprehensible terms for those who are relative novices to this area of church history. A great tool for both individual study and corporate reflection.

MICHAEL A. G. HAYKIN
Chair and Professor of Church History
Southern Baptist Theological Seminary
Louisville, Kentucky

Christianity is an ancient religion, and Christians have long summed up their faith in the Word of God through the use of creeds and confessions. The creeds especially excel in setting forth our triune God: the Father, the Son, and the Holy Spirit. In this short and accessible study, Nate Pickowicz helpfully brings ancient truth to the modern reader for the glory of God the Trinity and for the buttressing and augmenting of our faith.

JOEL R. BEEKE
President, Puritan Reformed Theological Seminary
Grand Rapids, Michigan

This book admirably occupies a sweet spot of three happy convergences: author, topic, and potential readers. Nate Pickowicz adds this to his several previous worthy titles. His topic of early Christian creeds is critically important for promoting unity among believers and strengthening our commitment to orthodoxy. His potential readership will appreciate his straightforward and pastoral manner. In *Christ & Creed*, Pickowicz ably expounds the subject without swamping interested newbies. Having read it closely, I heartily commend it to you with expectant prayers for your edification in our most holy and ancient faith.

D. Scott Meadows
Pastor, Calvary Baptist Church (Reformed)
Exeter, New Hampshire

When I was saved out of false doctrine it was the gospel that did it, but once saved I faced the tall task of sifting through the wreckage of twisted beliefs. What is true? What have real Christians believed for ages? What is doctrinally accurate? How do I test supposed new revelations from self-proclaimed prophets and apostles? Creeds! Faithful forerunners have fought the fight, run their race, and left helpful, doctrinal 'checkpoints' for us today. Nate Pickowicz has put them all in this book for you. I know you will be blessed!

Costi W. Hinn
Teaching Pastor, Shepherd's House Bible Church
Founder and President, For the Gospel
Chandler, Arizona

CHRIST & CREED

CREED

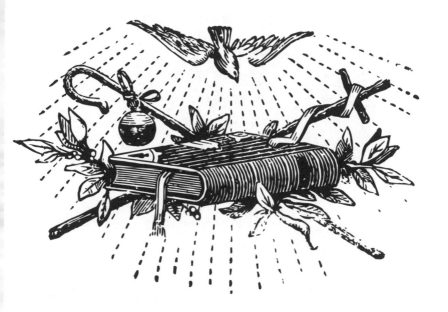

The Early Church Creeds & their Value for Today

NATE PICKOWICZ

CHRISTIAN
FOCUS

Scripture quotations are from The Holy Bible, English Standard Version, copyright © 2001 by Crossway Bibles, a publishing ministry of Good News Publishers. Used by permission. All rights reserved.

All creeds and confessions are quoted from *Creeds, Confessions, & Catechisms: A Reader's Edition* edited by Chad Van Dixhoorn, Wheaton: Crossway, 2022, except for the Second Helvetic Confession, which is quoted from *Reformed Confessions Harmonized*, edited by Joel R. Beeke & Sinclair B. Ferguson, Grand Rapids: Baker Books, 1999.

paperback ISBN 978-1-5271-1040-3
ebook ISBN 978-1-5271-1073-1

10 9 8 7 6 5 4 3 2 1

Published in 2023
by
Christian Focus Publications Ltd.,
Geanies House, Fearn, Ross-shire
IV20 1TW, Great Britain.

www.christianfocus.com

Cover design by Rubner Durais

Printed and bound by
Bell and Bain Glasgow

Contents

This book is dedicated to Dustin Benge,
my friend for all time and a lover of the truth.

1

Why Do We Need Creeds?

The Bible is the Word of God.

This one truth undergirds every component of the Christian life. The Bible is the scriptural revelation of truth from the mouth of God. Everything we are meant to know *from* God regarding the Christian faith has been given to us *by* God in the form of Holy Scripture. With regard to divine revelation, nothing can be added to it, nor taken away (see Rev. 22:18–19).

We affirm that the Bible is *inspired* by God (2 Tim. 3:16; 2 Pet. 1:19–21), meaning that He spoke forth words which were written down for us. We affirm that the Bible is *inerrant* (Ps. 119:160; John 17:17; Titus 1:2; Heb. 6:18), meaning that it is completely without errors or falsehoods in the original manuscripts. We affirm that the Bible is *authoritative* (Josh. 1:8; Isa. 40:8; Matt. 5:17–19), meaning that God vests the Scripture with his own binding authority, so that when Scripture speaks God speaks. We also affirm that the Bible is *sufficient* for us (2 Tim. 3:17; cf. Ps. 19:7–14), meaning that it provides everything we need for life and practice.[1]

---

1. For further reading on the doctrine of Scripture, see R.C. Sproul, *Knowing Scripture* (Downers Grove: InterVarsity Press, 2009) and Robert Saucy, *Scripture: Its Power, Authority, and Relevance* (Nashville: Word Publishing, 2001).

At the heart of the Protestant Reformation was the battle over the authority and sufficiency of the Bible. The Roman Catholic Church, although they regarded the Bible as wholly authoritative, they also looked to other forms of authority (church councils, tradition, rulings from popes) as equally authoritative. The Reformers, however, maintained the distinction that Scripture alone (*sola Scriptura*) was the supremely authoritative standard by which all must be finally resolved in the Christian life. But what the Reformers were *not* advocating was a total rejection of all extra-biblical teaching. They saw the value of the writings of the early church fathers, as well as many of the old ecumenical creeds. These things were profitable, so far as they were dependent on the Word of God.

There are many today who, in the name of '*sola Scriptura*,' completely reject any and all historical Christian documents out of the fear of abandoning the Bible. We hear phrases today like 'No creed but the Bible!' or 'No creed but Christ!' The thrust of these kinds of general sentiments is that we do not need any other writings—we only need the Bible to live a vibrant Christian life. On the necessity and sufficiency of the Bible, I would add my hearty 'AMEN!' The Bible alone, along with the illuminated understanding given by the Holy Spirit, is all that is needed for salvation and sanctification.

However, I believe that 'No creed but Christ' misses the mark. This is not because Christ and His Word are insufficient. Rather it is that the sentiment conveys the notion that *all* other historical Christian writings (creeds, confessions, catechisms, etc.) are not profitable or helpful, or even that they should not be used at all. Furthermore, it misses the fact that the Holy Spirit has worked in the minds of believers in years past to give them illumination and understanding. To ignore their testimony is to ignore the history of the ministry of the

Spirit. Sadly, many believers live their entire lives completely disconnected from the rich Christian heritage and helpful blessings of such treasures.

In fact, I was one of them.

CREEDLESS CHRISTIANITY

I grew up in a small, rural church in New Hampshire. Our family attended church every Sunday, yet I never once recall hearing any kind of creed or confession recited or taught. If you would have pressed me on it, I could not have told you even one thing that anyone in church history had contributed, let alone the early creeds. In fact, I didn't even know such things existed until I was an adult. Furthermore, if any kind of creedal or confessional language was taught in seminary, I don't remember it. When I was ordained as a minister in our baptistic tradition, I was not required to subscribe to any specific early creed or Protestant confession. In other words, this whole creedal world had been foreign to me for most of my life as a Christian.

However, when I began to preach and teach the Bible, I found myself desiring to express the truth of Christianity in short, understandable ways. As I began to bump into the language of the creeds, I found that they helped me both articulate the truth of what I was trying to communicate, as well as keep me from committing unintentional theological errors. I remember teaching on the person of Jesus Christ and wanting to succinctly express how we understand the relationship of his two natures. I stumbled onto the Definition of Chalcedon which articulated that Jesus is 'truly God and truly man.' After doing a little more study of the phrase and its implications, I adopted the verbiage for whenever I spoke of the two natures of Christ. Creedal language saved me from making a theological and Christological error.

As I began to investigate more, I started to see the value of reading and studying creeds. They offered me both helpful language to articulate my faith and confidence that I was not operating outside of the orthodox beliefs of the church since the days of the apostles, but wrapping my mind around all of this felt overwhelming—and I don't think I'm alone. For Christians who grow up in churches that recite and teach creeds and confessions, embracing this material feels almost second nature; but to 'non-creedal believers'—if I may generalize—tackling all of this can be daunting. Yet I believe that what the early church held as orthodox can only help us if we devote ourselves to the study of the early creeds and confessions.

WHAT IS A CREED?

Our English word 'creed' is derived from the Latin word *credo* which means 'I believe.' Regardless of how short or long, it is a statement of personal faith. However, the early church used the Greek word *symbolon* (where we get our word 'symbol') to refer to creeds. In essence, *symbolon* refers to two pieces placed side by side for comparison. One piece was verified for its authenticity if it matched the corresponding piece sitting next to it. This is helpful for us when we consider the usefulness of creeds. A creed functions as a comparative symbol to the grander body of truth to which it corresponds. In other words, a creed represents a small part of the whole Christian faith. How so?

In order to understand the Christian faith completely, one would have to be able to read, study, understand, compile, and synthesize the entire Bible in order to affirm it. A creed, however, provides us with essential Christian truth in shorthand. Speaking about both creeds and confessions, Carl Trueman notes that they 'represent a public statement of what a particular church or denomination believes that Scripture teaches in a synthetic form.' To be even more succinct, they are 'a thematic summary of what the Bible teaches.'[2] Beyond this, Philip Schaff adds that creeds are 'a form of words setting forth with authority certain articles of belief, which are regarded by the framers as necessary for salvation, or at least for the well-being of the Christian Church.'[3]

Earlier on, I made mention of believers who hold to 'No Creed but Christ' as their core conviction. The irony is that statement is itself a creedal statement. It carries with it a whole host of beliefs about orthodoxy and how it is passed down from generation to generation. What is ironic is that, in many cases, many modern churches that reject creeds will still feature doctrinal statements on their websites, which is nothing more than a modern confession! I am inclined to believe, therefore, that the issue is not as much with offering up written statements of belief as it is rejecting the perception that somehow the man-made documents handed down to us through church history are an affront to our firm belief in the supremacy of the Word of God.

And so, we must then ask the question: Does the Bible affirm the use of creeds? Are there examples of creedal statements in Scripture? What does God think about all of this? You might be surprised by what you find.

THE BIBLE'S USE OF CREEDS

The Bible makes use of a number of statements that are creedal in nature. Both Old and New Testaments include various forms of creeds. In the Old Testament we read of several creedal statements that were memorized and recited by the people of Israel. Two of the more prominent ones are found in

---

2. Carl Trueman, *The Creedal Imperative* (Wheaton: Crossway, 2012), 17.

3. Philip Schaff, *The Creeds of Christendom* (1931; republished, Grand Rapids: Baker Books, 2007), I:4–5.

Exodus 13:14–15, a call to instruct future generations on the purpose of the Passover, and what is known as the *Shema* from Deuteronomy 6:4–6, a confession designed 'to cement Israel's collective conviction that Yahweh was to be the sole object of their adoration, affection, and allegiance.'[4]

In the New Testament we see several statements that scholars believe are early church creeds. For instance, five times in Paul's letters he makes reference to a 'trustworthy saying.' We read in 1 Timothy 1:15, 'Christ Jesus came into the world to save sinners, of whom I am the foremost.' Variations of this sentiment are repeated over and over again throughout the Scriptures, as it functions as the core belief in the gospel. In 2 Timothy 2:11–13 Paul offers a longer creedal statement:

> If we have died with him, we will also live with him; if we endure, we will also reign with him; if we deny him, he also will deny us; if we are faithless, he remains faithful—for he cannot deny himself.

This statement pertains to the confession of believers who endure suffering for the cause of Christ. Other 'trustworthy statements' are found in 1 Timothy 3:1 and 4:7–9, as well as Titus 3:4–8.

One early New Testament confession is made by the apostle Peter in Matthew 16:16, where he declares of Jesus, 'You are the Christ, the Son of the living God.' Some have even dubbed this statement as 'The Great Confession.' Philip Schaff notes, 'This naturally became substance of the baptismal confession, since Christ is the chief object of the Christian faith.'[5] While Schaff maintains that this one confession became the backbone of what

---

4. J.V. Fesko, *The Need for Creeds Today: Confessional Faith in a Faithless Age* (Grand Rapids: Baker Academic, 2020), 5.

5. Schaff, *The Creeds of Christendom*, I:6.

was later developed into the Apostles' Creed, Peter's confession truly is the heart confession of every Christian believer.

The simplest and most profound creed coming out of the New Testament is this: 'Jesus is Lord.' At a time when Roman citizens were commanded to profess Caesar as lord, Christians could literally lose their lives for declaring the fundamental truth that 'Jesus is Lord.' Yet we see in several places in the New Testament instructions for how and why this confession was made. Paul tells the Roman believers, in his letter to them, 'if you confess with your mouth that Jesus is Lord and believe in your heart that God raised him from the dead, you will be saved' (Rom. 10:9). In this way, the confession of the lordship of Christ demonstrates saving faith within the heart. Of course, no one can fake such genuine faith, which is why Paul elsewhere conveys, 'no one can say "Jesus is Lord," except in the Holy Spirit' (1 Cor. 12:3). Saving faith is Spirit-wrought faith which manifests itself in Christian confession. Beyond this, however, Paul tells of the day when Christ returns in glory, 'every knee should bow,' he writes, 'and every tongue confess that *Jesus Christ is Lord*, to the glory of God the Father' (Phil. 2:10–11, emphasis added). This one confession, however short it is, is the persistent confession of every believer from the time of Christ's first advent to the time of his second coming.

Perhaps the earliest creed recorded in the New Testament comes in 1 Corinthians 15:3–4 where Paul reminds the church of the summation of the message that he delivered to them which was 'of first importance,' which was 'that Christ died for our sins in accordance with the Scriptures, that he was buried, that he was raised on the third day in accordance with the Scriptures.' Of its existence as a popular creed, Paul made note of the fact that 'I delivered to you…what I also received' (v. 3), meaning that the content of the confession had been passed down through teaching. What a glorious truth! one that would have been recited by believers all throughout the Roman Empire, as it serves as a summary of the essential elements of the gospel. Yet, as Tony Costa notes, 'Any gospel message that does not have the death, burial, and resurrection of Jesus is no gospel at all but is rather "another gospel" which comes under the anathema of God (Gal. 1:6–9).'[6]

Beyond the creeds and confessional statements actually quoted in the pages of Scripture, we also read imperatives in the New Testament that call for the use of sound doctrinal statements. In his letter to his younger disciple, Timothy, Paul instructs him to 'follow the pattern of the sound words that you have heard from me, in the faith and love that are in Christ Jesus' (2 Tim. 1:13). The idea being that Timothy was to follow a prescribed pattern of speaking and teaching doctrine which aligns with the things that he had been taught from Paul. This implies that Timothy is going to have to conform his own words and phrases to 'a form of sound words' which describes 'a model, form, or standard that is intended to function as a trustworthy or reliable guide.'[7]

Elsewhere, in Titus 2:1, Paul tells another of his disciples to 'teach what accords with sound doctrine.' Again, this suggests that whatever Titus says in his teaching, it must conform to a category of sound doctrine established by Paul. His words have to align and be found to be orthodox. This is more than simply permission to speak freely with guardrails. As Carl Trueman notes, 'the Bible itself seems to demand that we have forms of sound words, and that is what creeds are.'[8] We are called to make use of tools that can help us maintain doctrinal

---

6. Tony Costa, *Early Christian Creeds and Hymns—What the Earliest Christians Believed in Word and Song: An Exegetical and Theological Study* (Peterborough: H&E Academic, 2021), 43.

7. Carl Trueman has a helpful discussion of this concept in *The Creedal Imperative* (Wheaton: Crossway, 2012), 72–79.

8. Trueman, *The Creedal Imperative*, 76.

orthodoxy. But of course, everything that is written by human hands must be in full subordination to Holy Scripture. Even the Westminster Confession of Faith (1:10) expresses such subordination:

> The supreme judge by which all controversies of religion are to be determined, and all decrees of councils, opinions of ancient writers, doctrines of men, and private spirits, are to be examined, and in whose sentence we are to rest, can be no other but the Holy Spirit speaking in the Scripture.[9]

Therefore, only Scripture is conscience-binding. But if the Bible makes use of creeds, then we too should consider the value of using them ourselves.

THE VALUE OF CREEDS

As we consider the use of creeds, it may be helpful to think through the value they provide for us as believers. After all, we are never commanded to use any specific creed, but we are commanded to align our understanding of God with his revealed truth. However, our historic creeds are valuable to us for several key reasons.

1. Creeds Summarize Christian Truth

Unless you have memorized the entire Bible and are able to instantly recall and synthesize the verses together to form doctrine, then you rely on summaries of biblical truth to wrap your arms around what you believe. For example, the phrase 'Jesus Christ died on the cross to pay for sins' is a succinct summary of verses like Matthew 20:28, John 3:16, John 10:11, Romans 5:8–10, 1 Corinthians 15:3, 2 Corinthians 5:14–15, 1 Thessalonians 5:10, Hebrews 2:9, 1 Peter 3:18, along with

---

9. westminsterstandards.org/westminster-confession-of-faith/

about a hundred others. However, we don't recite every single verse when we want to testify to Christ's saving work; rather we employ the use of a summary statement. And that's what creeds do for us. They summarize essential truth in succinct ways so that we can clearly and accurately communicate what we believe the Bible says about any point of doctrine.

2. Creeds Testify to What the Church has Always Believed

Another benefit of creeds is that they demonstrate to us what generations of Christians who have lived before us have believed. The simple fact that something is old does not make it true (for example, see the horrendous 'Gnostic Gospels' of the third and fourth centuries!). But when millions of Christians from around the world, over hundreds of years, have uniformly affirmed statements like the Apostles' Creed, the Nicene Creed, or the Athanasian Creed, it quickly becomes clear that to ignore or reject those statements would be extremely foolish. Furthermore, studying what early Christians affirmed, often at the cost of their own lives, is valuable for us and can encourage us in our faith. We do not believe what we believe in a vacuum. There are timeless truths that have been affirmed throughout church history and we would do well to know them.

3. Creeds Help Us Be Precise in How We Express Truth

One of the challenges of growing in the Christian faith is learning how to speak and think in Christian language— as we already read, to 'teach what accords with sound doctrine' (Titus 2:1). Our gospel testimony is conveyed to others primarily through words, and it is God's Word itself that minister to us. And so, if sound *words* matter to the Lord, they should certainly matter to us. The language of Christian creeds has been carefully, studiously, and prayerfully crafted to express the truth of Scripture accurately. And while the writing of the creeds was done by humans who can err, they have withstood the test of time and have proven helpful for countless believers who desire to express their faith with precise words.

4. Creeds Help Us Guard Against Heresy and Error

Creeds not only help us convey Christian truth with precise language, they also help guard us from affirming doctrinal heresy. The early ecumenical church councils that produced the Nicene Creed and the Definition of Chalcedon were responding to serious doctrinal errors that threatened Christianity. Many of the creeds were written to contend for various points of doctrine, and to protect the truth of the Word of God. As we will later see, even heretics use Scripture, but the faithful work done by countless Christian teachers who came beforehand can help us rightly understand and apply the biblical text. When Christians affirm and adhere to these statements, they are standing in a long line of orthodox believers who reject historic heresies and affirm the timeless truth of the Christian faith.

5. Creeds Unify Believers Who Share the Same Testimony

Another benefit of holding to the truth of creeds is that it unites us with other faithful Christians throughout church history. The language of these documents captures the testimony of believers down through the ages, and when we affirm the same truths with the same words, we add our voices to theirs, in praise and adoration of our Lord. After all, the Bible says that 'there is one body and one Spirit—just as you were called to the one hope that belongs to your call—one Lord, one faith, one baptism, one God and Father of all, who is over all and through all and in all' (Eph. 4:4–6). This idea of 'one faith' means that every Christian believer maintains the same adherence to essential biblical truth, which is stated and summarized in the creeds we affirm. There is steadfast unity of all believers who affirm 'one faith' together for all time.

THE STRUCTURE OF THIS BOOK

The book you hold in your hands is a high-level overview and exposition of the early church creeds. It is certainly not meant to be exhaustive. I have chosen to keep it digestible for those who are either new to creeds or who simply desire a brush-up.

Chapters 2 through 5 offer surveys of the early major ecumenical creeds, namely the Apostles' Creed, the Nicene Creed, the Definition of Chalcedon, and the Athanasian Creed. Each chapter will provide a historical introduction followed by some helpful comments on the content of the creed. As you will see, the early creeds tend to build on one another, so my comments on the later creeds will address more of the distinctiveness of the successive creeds and will not rehash the truths previously explained in earlier chapters. While there are various iterations of these creeds throughout history that I do not mention, my goal was to work mainly with the key documents of the early church.

In Chapter 6 we take a bird's-eye look at how the essential doctrine of the early church creeds is expressed in the Protestant confessions of the sixteenth and seventeenth centuries. Due to the limitations of this book, however, we will not be able to survey every confession individually. Instead, it will only touch on the key confessions' teaching on the doctrines of Christ and the Trinity. Chapter 7 will briefly examine the implications of essential Christian doctrine against several of the more popular errors of today.

As we progress, it is my earnest prayer that this study would help you develop more clear and sound language with which to articulate what you believe and connect you to a long history of orthodox Christian believers who have gone before us, declaring the glorious truths of our saving faith in Jesus Christ.

2

The Apostles' Creed

One of the most universally recognized and accepted creeds in church history is no doubt what has come to be known as the Apostles' Creed. For centuries, it has been recited widely, confessed boldly, and believed sincerely. J.I. Packer observes, 'If life is a journey, then the million-word-long Holy Bible is the large-scale map with everything in it, and the hundred-word Apostles' Creed...is the simplified road map.'[1] Additionally, R.C. Sproul notes, 'It boldly declares that there is truth that is foundational to life, a truth that cannot be compromised without the peril of falling into the abyss of meaninglessness.'[2] But where did it come from? Why is it so popular?

BACKGROUND

The origins of the Apostles' Creed are a bit mysterious. One early tradition, according to an Italian Christian writer named Rufinus, maintains that before the twelve apostles parted ways to carry the gospel to the farthest reaches of the known world, they gathered together and composed a short creed, each

---

1. J.I. Packer, *Growing in Christ* (Wheaton: Crossway, 1994), 17.

2. R.C. Sproul, *What We Believe: Understanding and Confessing the Apostles' Creed* (Grand Rapids: Baker Books, 2015), 10.

apostle contributing one line.[3] Most scholars regard this story as pure fiction, but it serves as the reason why the statement is called 'the Apostles' Creed.' The general consensus is that the creed was derived from the Old Roman Creed (*c.* A.D. 140) that was recited during baptisms.[4] However, the first written reference was made in a letter from Ambrose of Milan to Rome in A.D. 389. It continued to develop until it was formalized and accepted by the Western churches during the reign of Charlemagne sometime around the early ninth century.[5] Even today, it is recited in virtually every Roman Catholic diocese and Protestant denomination (though more in some denominations than others).

As for the name and content, Francis Turretin muses: 'The Apostles' Creed is so called, not efficiently (as delivered by the apostles), but materially (as it was drawn from the doctrines of the apostles and is the marrow and substance of them).'[6] Or put another way, 'The Apostles' Creed is the earliest attempt of the Christian mind to systematize the teachings of the Scripture, and is, consequently, the uninspired foundation upon which the whole after-structure of symbolic literature rests.'[7] In other words, the creed consists of the basic essentials of the Christian faith. It has been stated many times that, while you can certainly believe and affirm *more* than the Apostles' Creed, you cannot believe and affirm any *less*. William Perkins has said, it is 'indeed the very pith and substance of

---

3.   Donald Fairbairn and Ryan M. Reeves, *The Story of Creeds and Confessions: Tracing the Development of the Christian Faith* (Grand Rapids: Baker Academic, 2019), 19.

4.   Justin S. Holcomb, *Know the Creeds and Councils* (Grand Rapids: Zondervan, 2014), 25.

5.   Carl Trueman, *The Creedal Imperative* (Wheaton: Crossway, 2012), 89.

6.   Francis Turretin, *Institutes of Elenctic Theology.* George Musgrave Giger, trans., James T. Dennison, Jr., ed. (Phillipsburg: P&R Publishing, 1992), 1:61.

7.   William G.T. Shedd cited in Philip Schaff, ed. *The Creeds of Christendom* (1931, repr.; Grand Rapids: Baker Books, 2007), I:16.

Christian religion.'[8] So essential is the content of Apostles' Creed, the theologian Herman Witsius remarked, 'the [person] who wantonly rejects it, ought not to be esteemed a Christian.'[9] It is nothing short of the expression of core Christianity.

What is contained in the Apostles' Creed? While scholars have produced countless pages of commentary on the content of the creed, the following brief exposition may be helpful to get at the heart of its teaching.

THE APOSTLES' CREED

As mentioned earlier, the creed begins with the statement 'I believe' (Latin: *credo*). The creed's content is not just meant to be understood or affirmed, but conscientiously believed to the core of one's own soul. This is the heart cry of every genuine Christian believer. As to its structure, the creed consists of four main parts: God, Christ, the Spirit, and the Church.

I believe in God the Father Almighty, Maker of heaven and earth. The first line of the creed identifies the core of belief in the person of God. This identifies Christianity as a God-focused religion, over and against so many of the self-focused religions of the world. But even more distinct than other religions who claim to worship a god, the creed identifies 'God the Father'—a personal title for God given in the Bible (Deut. 32:6; Matt. 5:48; Eph. 1:3, etc.). Even in Jesus' model prayer, He instructed the disciples to begin by praying 'Our *Father* in heaven, hallowed be your name' (Matt. 6:9, emphasis added). More than just a distant god who keeps himself aloof from his creation, God the Father loves His people and treats us as children.

---

8. William Perkins, *The Works of William Perkins*: Volume 5. Ryan Hurd, ed. (Grand Rapids: Reformation Heritage Books, 2017), 4.

9. Herman Witsius, *Sacred Dissertations on the Apostles' Creed* (repr. Grand Rapids: Reformation Heritage Books, 2010), I:14.

The next phrase qualifies 'God the Father' in order to give us a greater understanding of His nature and attributes. He is called 'Almighty' who is the 'Maker of heaven and earth.' This not only speaks to God's creative abilities to bring forth all of existence besides Himself ('heaven and earth' no doubt representing the entire creation), but also the power by which He has created everything. While the creed doesn't articulate every one of God's many attributes, the fact that He is 'Almighty' is a way to represent them all (cf. 1 Chron. 29:11; Ps. 91:1–2; Jer. 32:17; Rom. 1:20, etc.).

I believe in Jesus Christ, his only-begotten Son, our Lord;

At this point in the creed, we are introduced to the person of Jesus Christ. The name 'Jesus' refers to Him who was born to Mary in Bethlehem more than two thousand years ago, while 'Christ' comes from the Greek word *christos* which translates the Hebrew word rendered *Messiah* (meaning 'anointed one'). And so, 'Christ' is not a name but a title for the long-awaited Savior who had been promised to deliver God's people.

Following the identification of Jesus Christ, we read that he is called God's 'only-begotten Son.' This designation has been the cause of much controversy and misunderstanding through the years. While the full expression of the doctrine of the Trinity did not come until later years, the church's belief and apprehension of the deity of Jesus Christ has never been in question. Jesus is God (e.g. John 1:1–3; 20:28; Phil. 2:6–11; Col. 1:15–20; Titus 2:13). However, how do we understand Jesus in relation to God the Father? The Bible refers to Jesus as the *Son* of God—His 'only-begotten Son' (John 3:16, 18; 1 John 4:9). This is not to be understood as Jesus being somehow one son of many, or even that He came into existence at any one point. Rather it utilizes the Hebrew expression 'son of...' to refer to the comparative likeness of parents and children.

To be a 'son of' someone is to be regarded as being *just like* them, and to be 'begotten' is to come forth from them.[10] As an expression, Jesus as the 'son of God' is understood to reflect His identification as God (Luke 1:35; cf. Matt. 16:13–17), as well as to His position of preeminence (Heb. 1:5). Added to Jesus' title as God's *Son*, He is also His '*only*-begotten' Son (John 1:18)—there's no one else like Him.

The final title given to Jesus Christ in this line is that of 'Lord.' The word 'Lord' translates the Greek word *kurios* which means 'Master.' While the title was used as a way to address an honored person, the lordship of Christ refers to His absolute sovereignty and dominion over all things. In some cases, it was even used as a title of deity. More specifically, however, Christ here is called '*our* Lord,' referring to all believers who would affirm the truth of the creed. In this way we understand that Jesus is the reigning Lord over the life of every Christian believer, in this age and in the age to come (cf. Acts 2:36; Rom. 10:9; Col. 2:6). To acknowledge Jesus as Lord is to submit oneself to His mastery over every aspect of life and to confess His full deity.

Who was conceived by the Holy Spirit, born of the Virgin Mary;
The Old Testament prophesied that the Messiah would come by way of a virgin birth: 'Behold, the virgin shall conceive and bear a son, and shall call his name Immanuel' (Isa. 7:14). This was fulfilled at the birth of Jesus to the virgin Mary recorded in both Matthew and Luke's Gospels. The reason the virgin birth is significant is because it succeeds in bringing forth a 'second Adam' who came 'in the likeness of sinful flesh' (Rom. 8:3) to redeem what was lost at the fall of the first Adam.

---

10. An expanded discussion of 'begotten' occurs in Chapters 3, 4, and 5. For the translation of 'only-begotten' being preferred over 'one and only,' see the discussion in Chapter 3.

Yet Jesus was miraculously 'conceived of the Holy Spirit' and born to Mary while she was still a virgin. In this way, not only was Jesus' birth proof of His true and full humanity, but He was born without the stain of original sin (2 Cor. 5:21; Heb. 7:26; 1 Pet. 2:21–22). Furthermore, because Jesus was born without sin, and is Himself God incarnate, His death on the cross would surely be an acceptable sacrifice to God for the payment of sins, as a 'spotless Lamb' (Heb. 7:27; 1 Pet. 1:19; cf. John 1:29). Only a sinless sacrifice was able to be offered for the sins of God's people, and this was accomplished through the virgin birth.

Suffered under Pontius Pilate; was crucified, dead, and buried;
The next few lines are taken nearly verbatim from 1 Corinthians 15:3–4 where Paul notes that 'Christ died for our sins in accordance with the Scriptures, that he was buried, that he was raised on the third day in accordance with the Scriptures.' This line in the creed makes note of the first two aspects of Paul's testimony.

The crucifixion and death of Jesus Christ is the single most significant event in human history. All four Gospels recount the details of His suffering, trial, death, burial, and resurrection. The creed makes reference to the fact that Jesus 'suffered under Pontius Pilate,' who was the Roman magistrate over Israel at the time. This detail roots the crucifixion of Christ in history thus affirming its authenticity. Under his watch, Jesus was scourged and then crucified by being nailed to a wooden cross (Matt. 27:26–44).

After suffering the agony of the cross, Jesus 'yielded up his spirit' and died (Matt. 27:50; Mark 15:37; Luke 23:46; John 19:30). Why is it significant that Jesus died? It was the full payment of the sins of all believers (1 John 2:2; 4:10). His final words—'It is finished'—tell of His full satisfaction of the wrath of God against sin, as well as the ransom payment made for us (Mark 10:45; Rom. 3:25; Heb. 2:17).

After His death, the body of Jesus was taken down from the cross, and honorably prepared for burial by his followers (John 19:38–42). At that point, His body was laid in the tomb of Joseph of Arimathea (Matt. 27:57–61), as a fulfillment of the prophecy: '[he was] with a rich man in his death' (Isa. 53:9). Often times people will ask why Jesus had to die. His death effectively destroyed the eternal punishment for sin, as we read in Colossians 2:14, that His death 'cancel[ed] the record of debt that stood against us…this he set aside, nailing it to the cross.' Jesus' death ensures that whatever penalty was reserved for us for our sinfulness has been completely and utterly destroyed on the cross, and given a complete burial, never to be revived again.

He descended into hell;
Many believers bristle against the line, 'he descended into hell,' for various reasons. Part of the reason is because the Roman Catholic Church has used it to justify the notion that Christ descended into the depths of hell to fight for the souls of departed saints. This opens the door for the notion of purgatory, which is foreign to Scripture. However, one supposed proof text for this interpretation comes from the highly debated text, 1 Peter 3:18–19, where we read that Christ 'being put to death…he went and proclaimed to the spirits in prison,' that they might repent of their disobedience to God and be redeemed. Some scholars have argued that the phrase is absent from the early versions of the creed, and therefore conclude that it doesn't belong. Others, however, have been able to identify the clause in early literature, thus strengthening the case for its authenticity. Nevertheless, there is an even greater problem with this interpretation of the creed. The Roman Catholic

interpretation that Christ ministered savingly to persons in hell seems to imply that the sacrificial death of Christ on the cross was somehow insufficient to atone for all believers.

However, the Gospel accounts are clear that, as Jesus prepared to die on the cross, He announced, 'Father, into your hands I commit my spirit' (Luke 23:46). The very next moment, Christ was in heaven with the Father, not in hell with sinners. Furthermore, there is a theological reason why Jesus would not have gone to hell to preach the gospel to the dead. On the cross, Christ paid the debts of sinners in full. As we saw earlier, Jesus's final words recorded in John 19:30 were, 'It is finished!' The original Greek word used in the verse, *tetelestai*, means 'paid in full.' The death of Christ was the full and final payment for *all* sins, for *all* believers, for *all* time.

Many scholars make note of how the early church would have understood Christ's descent into hell. Second-century theologian Tertullian wrote that 'Christ our God, Who because He was man died according to the same Scriptures, satisfied this law also by undergoing the form of human death in the underworld.'[11] Chrysostom refers to death as 'the lower parts of the earth.'[12] In other words, 'descended into hell' is another way of referring to death and burial in the ground. Add to that, as Justin Holcomb notes, the Latin translations of the creed have employed the phrases *ad inferna* ('into hell') and *ad infernos* ('to the dead') to refer to Christ's descent.[13] Most assuredly, the creed is not intending to convey the notion that Christ's death was some mystical, spiritual occurrence, but a literal, bodily death whereby he was buried in a tomb, into 'the lower parts of the earth' where He remained three days until resurrecting.

---

11. Quoted in Holcomb, *Know the Creeds and Councils*, 28.

12. Quoted in Witsius, *Sacred Dissertations on the Apostles' Creed*, II:139.

13. Holcomb, *Know the Creeds and Councils*, 28.

The third day he arose again from the dead;

After being crucified and buried, the Bible tells us that, on the third day, Jesus rose from the grave (e.g. Matt. 16:21; 1 Cor. 15:3–4). In doing so, Jesus proved that He had conquered death once for all. Furthermore, as Mark Jones notes, 'The resurrection was the Triune God's 'Amen' to all that Christ did on earth as mediator, particularly through his vicarious sin-bearing death on the cross.'[14] Plainly stated, without the resurrection of Jesus Christ there is no salvation and no gospel.

More than a mere affirmation of the satisfaction of the Father's plan for salvation, Christ's resurrection also accomplishes work in the lives of believers. First, Christ's resurrection ensures the regeneration of believers, as 1 Peter 1:3 notes that '[God's] great mercy...has caused us to be born again to a living hope through the resurrection of Jesus Christ from the dead.' Second, Christ's resurrection ensures our justification: 'Jesus our Lord...was delivered up for our trespasses and raised for our justification' (Rom. 4:25). Third, Christ's resurrection ensures our future bodily resurrection. The apostle Paul notes, 'God raised the Lord and will also raise us up by his power' (1 Cor. 6:14). Fourth, Christ's resurrection empowers us to live righteously. 'For the death [Christ] died he died to sin, once for all, but the life he lives he lives to God. So you also must consider yourselves dead to sin and alive to God in Christ Jesus' (Rom. 6:10–11; cf. Rom. 8:11–13). In other words, the resurrection of Jesus Christ brings new life to all those who believe, in this life and in the life to come.

He ascended into heaven, and sits at the right hand of God the Father Almighty;

Forty days after Jesus' resurrection, the Bible teaches that He then ascended bodily up into the clouds (Acts 1:9). Scripture

---

14. Mark Jones, *Knowing Christ* (Edinburgh: The Banner of Truth Trust, 2015), 161.

records that as the disciples watched Him ascend, two angels appeared and spoke to them, 'Men of Galilee, why do you stand looking into heaven? This Jesus, who was taken up from you into heaven, will come in the same way as you saw him go into heaven' (v. 11). Not only was Jesus' ascension to complete the mission of journeying from heaven to earth and back to heaven, it also pointed to a greater prophecy from Zechariah 14:4 that the Messiah would return and 'his feet shall stand on the Mount of Olives' at the time of His second advent.

However, this ascent back to heaven is more than simply the completion of a journey—it is the exaltation of Jesus Christ as Sovereign Lord (Phil. 2:8–11). Furthermore, Christ's ascension begins the present priestly work of intercession in heaven (known as his 'session'), whereby He entered 'into heaven itself, now to appear in the presence of God on our behalf' (Heb. 9:24; cf. 4:14, 7:26). Now, Christ sits in the place of preeminence—'at the right hand of God the Father Almighty'—continuing to advocate for us and minister on our behalf before God. In this way, through the ministry of the Spirit, the Lord is able to intercede for the church according to the will of God (Rom. 8:27).

From there he shall come to judge the living and the dead.
At the end of Christ's current session in heaven, the Bible teaches that Christ will return to earth, as the creed states, 'to judge the living and the dead.' Older English versions of the creed use the word 'quick' to mean 'living.' In several places we read about the return of Christ where 'the Son of Man [comes] on the clouds of heaven with power and great glory' (Matt. 24:30), yet He comes 'in righteousness [to] judge and make war' (Rev. 19:11).

At His first coming, Jesus did not come to judge the world but to save it (John 3:17). However, His second coming has been designated specifically for the judgment of the unrighteous. Jesus declares, 'The Father judges no one, but has given all judgment to the Son' (John 5:22). This final judgment will not just be for those who are alive at the time of His coming ('the living'), but also for those who have passed on ('the dead'). The notion conveyed here is that no one is able to escape the judgment of Christ (Heb. 9:27). However, while unbelievers are condemned on the last day (Rev. 20:11–15), those who have been redeemed in Christ will be judged in righteousness and rewarded based on what they had done for Christ (1 Cor. 3:12–15).

I believe in the Holy Spirit;

In rounding out the Trinitarian declaration of the creed, this line affirms belief in the person of the Holy Spirit. The Bible clearly teaches the full deity of the Spirit as a member of the Godhead (e.g. Acts 5:3–4; 2 Cor. 13:14). In the beginning, the Spirit was active with the Father in the creation of all things (Gen. 1:2; cf. Ps. 104:30). The Spirit also shares with the Father and the Son all the divine attributes, including omniscience (1 Cor. 2:11), omnipresence (Ps. 139:7–10), omnipotence (Job 33:4), wisdom (Isa. 40:13), and truthfulness (1 John 5:6). The Bible also credits the Spirit with its own inspiration (2 Tim. 3:16–17). We read in 2 Peter 1:21 that 'no prophecy [of Scripture] was ever produced by the will of man, but men spoke from God as they were carried along by the Holy Spirit.'

Before He went to the cross, the Lord Jesus promised that He would send the Spirit to the disciples as a 'Helper' (John 14:16)—one who would minister to them. However, Jesus' enigmatic words that the Spirit would not only be *with* them but *in* them (v. 17), would be fully realized at the Spirit's arrival at Pentecost as the disciples in Jerusalem are spiritually indwelled (Acts 2:1–6ff). Why did this take place? Earlier in John's Gospel Jesus told Nicodemus, 'Truly, truly, I say to you, unless one is born of water and the Spirit, he cannot enter the kingdom of God' (John 3:5). This new birth is what is known as *regeneration*—a recreation of the human spirit (cf. Ezek. 36:26–28). The Spirit's indwelling presence and regenerating power is what applies the work of Christ in salvation to the believer (Eph. 1:13–14). Without the Spirit's work, personal salvation is impossible.

In addition to His creating, inspiring, and saving ministry, the Spirit also brings about the life-changing work of *sanctification*—growth in Christlikeness. This powerful work is evidenced by certain visible spiritual fruit like 'love, joy, peace, patience, kindness, goodness, faithfulness, gentleness, self-control' (Gal. 5:22–23). In this way, the Spirit strives with us to give us spiritual understanding (1 Cor. 2:10–16), convict us of our sins (John 16:8), endows us with gifts (1 Cor. 12:7, 11), and conform us into the image of Christ (Rom. 8:29, 12:1–2). And so, to 'believe in the Holy Spirit' is to acknowledge His full deity and His vital ministry in the life of every Christian believer.

The holy catholic church; the communion of saints;

This line is one of the more controversial sentiments in the creed, especially for modern Evangelical believers. It is an affirmation of belief in 'the holy catholic Church.' Many Protestants today bristle at this affirmation because they believe that it is an endorsement of the Roman Catholic Church. However, another definition of the word 'catholic' is *universal*. Justin Holcomb goes a step further, noting, 'Catholic' means the church exists in every nation where the gospel has spread,' citing the words of Ignatius of Antioch: 'wherever Jesus Christ is, there is the Catholic Church.'[15]

---

15. Holcomb, *Know the Creeds and Councils*, 29.

But this leads us to ask: *what is the church?* The Greek word translated 'church' in the Bible is *ekklesia*, which is generally understood to refer to the gathered assembly of Christian believers. Furthermore, the Bible describes 'the church' as 'the body of Christ' (Eph. 1:22–23; Col. 1:18), of which every regenerate believer is a member (1 Cor. 12:12–27). Peter goes a step further and calls the church, 'a chosen race, a royal priesthood, a holy nation, a people for [God's] own possession' (1 Pet. 2:9).

With regard to the word 'holy,' we understand that those whom God has chosen to redeem are therefore set apart and called out of the domain of darkness (Col. 1:13–14). The Greek word for 'saint' is *hagios* which refers to God's act of setting apart and purifying His people for His own divine purposes. And so, in this way, the church is 'the communion of saints'— the gathered assembly of Christian believers around the world. To affirm this part of the creed is to admit that, while Christians are redeemed by Christ individually, they are gathered together corporately and make up one united body (Eph. 4:4; cf. 1 Cor. 12:4ff).

The forgiveness of sins;
Christianity is not primarily a scheme for effecting social change or championing a better earthly life, although these can sometimes be additional results of its influence. It is, however, God's divine plan for reconciling fallen humanity to Himself. Adam and Eve committed the first sin in the Garden of Eden and were cursed by God as a result (Gen. 3:1–19). This curse extended to all humanity, as all people who would be born from their first parents would inherit that guilt and sin nature (cf. Rom. 5:12, 18–19; Eph. 2:1–3). The Bible is clear that God's only response to the violation of his holy commands is punishment by death (Rom. 6:23). And since 'all have sinned

and fall short of the glory of God' (Rom. 3:23; cf. 10–18), unless God intervenes, humanity is destined for hell.

However, even before the foundations of the world, God had planned a way of salvation for sinners. Without impugning His own character or violating His own justice, God provided a means by which sins could be paid for—through atonement. In the Old Testament we see animal sacrifice presented as a prefigurement of the atonement that would ultimately be made by Jesus Christ. The Bible affirms that 'everything is purified with blood, and without the shedding of blood there is no forgiveness of sins' (Heb. 9:22). However, it was not possible through the blood sacrifice of animals (Heb. 10:4), but only through the perfect and acceptable sacrifice of Jesus Christ on the cross (Heb. 9:24–26). When this sacrifice was made, once for all time (Heb. 10:11–12), then forgiveness of sins was made possible for God's people.

However, 'the forgiveness of sins' is not automatically granted to sinners. While the creed doesn't specify it, the confession of sins to God is certainly implied. In connection with 'the forgiveness of sins' is the need for *repentance*, which is a change of mind for the purpose of changing direction. More clearly, repenting of sins means that sorry sinners agree with God that His law has been violated, feel contrition and regret over the transgression, ask for forgiveness, and then purposes in their heart to obey God joyfully moving forward. Furthermore, 1 John 1:9 declares that 'if we confess our sins, [God] is faithful and just to *forgive* us our sins and to cleanse us from all unrighteousness' (emphasis added). It is only because of the sacrifice of Jesus Christ on our behalf that payment for sins has been made and forgiveness is given to us through faith.

The resurrection of the body;
Because of the curse of the fall, all people die physically—both believers and unbelievers. Yet Jesus Himself claims:

'I am the resurrection and the life. Whoever believes in me, though he die, yet shall he live, and everyone who lives and believes in me shall never die' (John 11:25–26). He embodied such a resurrection through His own raising from the dead on the third day. Because of the resurrection of Jesus Christ as 'the firstborn from the dead' (Col. 1:18; cf. Rev. 1:5), Christians who follow Him are also assured of a resurrection like his (1 Cor. 15:20–23). The promise of life after death is that God will bring us to heaven in new resurrected bodies.

The apostle Paul notes that 'flesh and blood cannot inherit the kingdom of God, nor does the perishable inherit the imperishable' (1 Cor. 15:50). This necessitates our resurrection, whereby, 'in a moment, in the twinkling of an eye, at the last trumpet. For the trumpet will sound, and the dead will be raised imperishable, and we shall be changed' (v. 52). However, our resurrection is not automatic. It comes because of Christ's own power and authority to raise us, as He proclaims in John 6:39–40, 'And this is the will of him who sent me, that I should lose nothing of all that he has given me, but raise it up on the last day. For this is the will of my Father, that everyone who looks on the Son and believes in him should have eternal life, and I will raise him up on the last day.' Our belief in the resurrection is truly a belief in the God who Himself resurrects us and brings us to heaven.

And the life everlasting. Amen.
The final line of the creed captures the hope of the future of every confessing Christian believer. While living in a fallen world because of sin, we join the creation in anxious longing for our physical redemption (Rom. 8:19–23). But what are we longing for? We do not merely desire a slightly modified version of our present life on earth—a life that is destined to come to an end. Instead, we long for a future life in the

new creation, which realizes the promise made in John 3:16, 'For God so loved the world, that he gave his only [begotten] Son, that whoever believes in him should not perish, *but have eternal life*' (emphasis added).

However, everlasting life is not itself the ultimate joy; rather the greatest hope of every believer is that we will always be with the Lord (1 Thess. 4:17). In the end, the longing for eternity is a desire to be with Jesus Christ. Paul tells the church, 'For you have died, and your life is hidden with Christ in God. When Christ who is your life appears, then you also will appear with him in glory' (Col. 3:3–4). And when we finally reside in the new creation with Christ, 'He will wipe away every tear from [our] eyes, and death shall be no more, neither shall there be mourning, nor crying, nor pain anymore' (Rev. 21:4). There will only be rejoicing in Christ.

The final word given in the creed is 'Amen,' which stands as a hearty affirmation of the truthfulness of what has been confessed.

3

The Nicene Creed

In echoing the theological consensus of Christian scholars worldwide, Lewis Ayres has noted that the Nicene Creed is 'the most important creed in the history of Christianity.'[1] What is the reason for its importance? Justin Holcomb aptly notes that 'it settled the question of how Christians can worship one God and also claim that this God is three persons.'[2] Furthermore, it gave the universal church both the understanding and language for how it can comprehend this divine mystery. It took the first step in solidifying the church's understanding of the relationship between the Father and the Son, as well as the place of the Spirit within the divine triad. History has borne witness to its veracity and timelessness, as the Nicene Creed holds the honorable title of being the first creed to obtain universal acceptance in the early church. But how did we get this wonderful creed?

BACKGROUND

When Constantine came into power in A.D. 324, he immediately took on the difficult task of trying to unite

---

1. Lewis Ayres, *Nicaea and its Legacy* (Oxford: Oxford University Press, 2004), 1.

2. Justin S. Holcomb, *Know the Creeds and Councils* (Grand Rapids: Zondervan, 2014), 33.

the Roman Empire. Persecution of the Christian church had been brought to a screeching halt in 313 with the issuing of the Edict of Milan, and now Christianity was beginning to enjoy freedom and flourishing in a whole new era. However, a bitter dispute between a presbyter named Arius (c. 256–336) and his bishop, Alexander of Alexandria, had ignited a controversy that threatened the fragile unity of the empire. While some have speculated that the dispute had to do in part with an ecclesiastical power play, the truth was that there were serious doctrinal issues at hand.

As early as 318, Arius began teaching that Jesus was not God, but only a created being who served the Most High. In his own words, Arius declared, 'He [the Son] possesses nothing proper...to God, in the real sense of propriety, for he is not equal to God, nor yet is he of the same substance... The Father is other than the Son in substance...because he is without beginning.'[3] In his own mind, Arius believed that he was preserving the uniqueness and dignity of God the Father, but did so at the expense of the Son and the Spirit. Alexander responded to Arius in a series of letters, critiquing his heretical position. Summarizing Alexander's theology, J.N.D. Kelly highlights: 'What he [Alexander] actually teaches is that the Son, as Son, is co-eternal with the Father, since God can never have been without His Word, His Wisdom, His Power, His Image, and the Father must always have been the Father.'[4] He declared Jesus to be God, not merely the one who would simply lead us to God, as was the popular Greek philosophy of the day. When Arius refused to surrender his position, Alexander publicly condemned him.

Emperor Constantine had been watching the war brewing between Alexander and Arius, and in 325 he moved to

---

3. Quoted in Ayres, *Nicaea and its Legacy*, 55.

4. J.N.D. Kelly, *Early Christian Doctrines*. Revised Edition (New York: HarperOne, 1978), 224.

assemble a council to deal with the issue, in order to attempt to preserve the unity and stability of the empire. On May 20, 325, approximately 220 bishops from all over the Roman Empire gathered in the city of Nicaea to form the first ecumenical council, presided over by Constantine himself. Attendees included Hosius of Corduba, Marcellus of Ancyra, Eusebius of Caesarea, and Alexander of Alexandria, along with his deacon, a promising young disciple named Athanasius.

For one month the council convened, hearing arguments, examining Scripture, and evaluating theological positions, including that of Arius. At the culmination of the council, they produced a new creed, aptly titled the Creed of Nicaea, which was modeled after many of the early Roman baptismal creeds. One key feature of the creed was the assertion that the Father and the Son possess the same divine *ousia* or 'substance.' However, in further distinguishing between orthodoxy and the false doctrine of the Arian party, the creed also included an anathema at its conclusion:

> But, those who say, Once he was not, or he was not before his generation, or became to be out of nothing, or who assert that he, the Son of God, is of a different *hypostasis* or *ousia*, or that he is a creature, or changeable, or mutable, the Catholic and Apostolic Church anathematizes them.[5]

When the new creed was ratified on June 19, 325, Arius refused to sign it, as it repudiated his position. At the council's conclusion, Arius' writings were condemned and he, along with his supporters, Theonas and Secundus, were exiled.

Unfortunately, the First Council of Nicaea did not effectively put an end to the Arian heresy. When Constantine

---

5. Quoted in Donald Fairbairn and Ryan M. Reeves, *The Story of Creeds and Confessions: Tracing the Development of the Christian Faith* (Grand Rapids: Baker Academic, 2019), 59.

died in 337 the empire de-stabilized and Arius' followers began to multiply. As Arianism resurfaced, Athanasius, the newly minted bishop of Alexandria, began to refute its errors, but the opposition was too great. New spiritual and political alliances proved to be too persuasive and Nicene theology was soon banished. Athanasius was sent into exile. In attempts to bridge the gap between feuding theological parties, a new party emerged who, out of a fear of being accused of modalism, rejected the Creed of Nicaea's declaration of Jesus being of the *same* substance as the Father (*homoousios*), embracing instead the notion of the Father and Son being of a *similar* substance (*homoiousios*). However, many of the adherents to this party eventually accepted *homoousios* once they realized that it was not a modalist claim, but a claim of the deity of Christ.

Athanasius died in 373, having fought for decades yet never realizing a theological victory. However, when Emperor Julian came to power in 361, he effectively ended all persecution of the Nicene party. In the wake of this reprieve, three key Cappadocian bishops took up the Nicene cause again: Basil of Caesarea, Gregory of Nazianzus, and Gregory of Nyssa. These post-Nicene scholars continued where Athanasius left off, as Harry Boer summarizes: 'The end result of seventy years of study, discussion, controversy, and political strife was the acceptance of Athanasius' one God in three persons and of the Cappadocians' three persons in one God. These were the two sides of the one confession of the Triune God.'[6] When pro-Nicene Emperor Theodosius took the throne in 379, he sought to root out Arianism once and for all. He convened a council of 150 bishops in Constantinople in 381 to reaffirm the theology of Nicaea, as well as expand the content of the Creed

---

6. Harry R. Boer, *A Short History of the Early Church* (Grand Rapids: Eerdmans, 1976), 119.

of Nicaea. The result is what we know as the Nicene Creed.[7] With the ratification of the new creed, Arianism and all its sister errors were anathematized for a final time.

THE NICENE CREED

The basic outline of the Nicene Creed is Trinitarian. While the words 'I believe' only appear in conjunction to the Father and the Spirit, the declaration is no doubt meant to be applied to each member of the Trinity: The Father Almighty, the Lord Jesus Christ, and the Holy Spirit. Many scholars who observe this format view the ministry of the church as an outpouring of the Spirit's work.

I believe in one God, the Father Almighty, Maker of heaven and earth, and of all things visible and invisible.

This opening line is virtually identical to that of the Apostles' Creed, with only the addition of the statement that God has created 'all things visible and invisible.' This addition is clearly drawn from Colossians 1:16, which incidentally, is attributed to the creative work of Jesus Christ. While this is certainly true of the work of the Father, the creed's purpose is to magnify the coequality of the Son, who shares in the creative acts of the Father (cf. John 1:3).

And in one Lord Jesus Christ, the only-begotten Son of God, begotten of the Father before all worlds;

This line begins the key portion of the creed which focuses on the person of Jesus Christ, who was the source of theological contention at both Nicaea and Constantinople. Who is Jesus? Is He God, or a created being? The Arians maintained that Jesus was created by God, while the Nicene theologians confessed

---

7. Because of the dominant influence of the Council of Constantinople on its development, many scholars refer to the Nicene Creed as the Niceno-Constantinopolitan Creed.

Jesus Christ to be God. In affirming His deity, they first began to expound on the Bible's teaching of His identity.

Scripture declares in several dozen places the distinctness of the Lord Jesus Christ (e.g. Acts 2:36; 10:36; Rom. 5:1, 11; 2 Cor. 13:14; Eph. 1:3; Phil. 3:20; etc.). The Greek word *kurios* can be translated generically as 'master,' but as a formal title, it is a specific reference to God. Furthermore, there is a linguistic connection between the reference to the 'one God, the Father Almighty' and the 'one Lord Jesus Christ.'[8] Again, not that Jesus is one of the creatures made by God, but wholly distinct *alongside* God. We see this conveyed in the beginning of John's Gospel: 'In the beginning was the Word, and the Word was with God, and the Word was God' (1:1). We know from verse 14 that 'the Word' who is with the Father in the beginning is none other than Jesus Christ.

The next phrase continues the biblical terminology about Jesus, calling Him 'the only-begotten Son of God.' Again, John's prologue says of Jesus that He is gloriously 'of the only [begotten] Son from the Father, full of grace and truth' (v. 14; cf. v. 18; 3:16, 18; 1 John 4:9). The Greek word translated 'only-begotten' is *monogenēs*, which generally refers to a person's only offspring. Some modern scholars maintain that this word means 'one and only' or 'one of a kind.'[9] This would affirm Jesus' utter uniqueness. However, the Nicene council no doubt had more in mind here, specifically, the Son's intimate and unique eternal relation to the Father—a concept further developed into what we now refer to as *eternal generation*.

Furthermore, the creed continues in asserting that Jesus is 'begotten of the Father before all worlds.' An older translation renders the last phrase, 'before all ages.' This solidifies that Jesus

---

8. Thomas F. Torrence, *The Trinitarian Faith: The Evangelical Theology of the Ancient Catholic Church*. Second Edition (London: T&T Clark, 1997), 117.

9. Merrill C. Tenney, *John* in *The Expositor's Bible Commentary*: Volume 9 (Grand Rapids: Zondervan, 1981), 33.

is not created in time by the Father, but preexistent with Him (cf. John 1:1–2). Up to this point, the Arians would have agreed with everything in the creed. While holding to the notion that Christ was a created being, Arius believed that He was not like other creatures, but a distinct intermediary between God and man.[10] In this way, Arius could still regard Jesus as being God's 'one and only Son'—totally unique—yet not Himself truly God. The next phrase undermines this completely.

God of God, Light of Light, very God of very God;
The next several phrases are meant to punctuate the creed, declaring repeatedly the Son's divine relation to the Father. Speaking distinctly of Jesus, the phrase 'God of God'[11] declares Him to be God—not of some other mystical or spiritual kind, but 'of God' the Most High. The phrase communicates the sameness between the Father and the Son. Scripture itself ascribes deity to the Son in many places. For example, Thomas declares Him to be 'My Lord and my God' (John 20:28) and Philippians 2:6 affirms that Jesus 'was in the form of God.' It is said of Jesus, 'in him the whole fullness of deity dwells bodily' (Col. 2:9) and the writer of Hebrews declares that Jesus 'is the radiance of the glory of God and the exact imprint of his nature' (Heb. 1:3), and so on. In every biblical reference made, Jesus is declared to be God… 'of God.'

To further accentuate the relation, the creed declares that Jesus is 'Light of Light.' Once again, in John's prologue, Jesus is called 'the light [that] shines in the darkness' (1:5). Furthermore, John the Baptist is said to have come to 'bear witness about the light' (1:7–9). To eliminate any question, Jesus, in John 8:12, declares Himself to be 'the Light of the world' (cf. 9:5; 12:35–36, 46). While the creed no doubt seizes

---

10. Torrence, *The Trinitarian Faith*, 118.

11. Some versions of the creed remove the phrase 'God of God' due to its seemingly redundant nature.

on the image of Jesus as 'Light,' the phrase also serves as an analogy that illustrates the impossibility of separating light from light itself. In the same way you cannot split a beam of light in two, you cannot separate God from God.

The third phrase in this rhythmic triad declares that Jesus is 'very God of very God.' The sense of 'very God' is that Jesus is *truly* God. In the same way Jesus often prefaced a serious statement with the words, 'truly, truly'—for emphasis—the creed further emphasizes the God-ness of Jesus by calling him 'very God of very God.' But how are we to understand the relationship of the Father and the Son?

Begotten, not made, being of one substance with the Father, by whom all things were made.

The next phrase repeats and emphasizes the eternality of Jesus as a non-created being. The creed reaffirms that He is 'begotten' of the Father, but 'not made' by the Father—a notion that did not originate with the Nicene theologians, but with Scripture (e.g. Acts 13:33; Heb. 5:5). This distinction points to the fact that Jesus is eternal. This stands in stark contradiction to Arius' belief: 'There once was a time when he [Jesus] was not.' Rather, Athanasius maintained, 'as the Father's attributes are everlastingness, immortality, eternity, and not being a creature, it follows that thus also we must think of the Son.'[12]

However, the council wrestled with how to articulate the exact relationship of the Father and the Son. The Creed of Nicaea employed the term *homoousios* (homo-oozy-oss), which means 'consubstantial' or 'of the *same* substance.' This means that the Son is of the same divine substance (or essence) as the Father. After Nicaea, however, rival heretical terms begin to pop up, the most popular sounding very similar to that used in the Creed of Nicaea, but with only one letter difference.

---

12. Quoted in Gregg R. Allison, *Historical Theology: An Introduction to Christian Doctrine* (Grand Rapids: Zondervan, 2011), 238.

The main competing view adopted the term *homoiousios* (homoy-oozy-oss)—'of a *similar* substance'—with regard to the Son's relation the Father. Compared to some of the more extreme views that arose after Nicaea, the *homoiousios* term seemed like an acceptable compromise, but the implications were still earth-shattering. This meant that the Son was only similar to the Father, but not essentially the same.

Scripture affirms the unity of the Father and the Son, as Jesus declared in John 10:30, 'I and the Father are one' (cf. John 17:22–23). But how do we understand the oneness between the Father and the Son? While they share the same *ousia* (substance or essence), there is a notable distinction between the two of them. This distinction will be further explained below in the discussion of the Spirit's relationship to the Father and the Son.

Who, for us men and for our salvation, came down from heaven and was incarnate by the Holy Spirit of the Virgin Mary, and was made man;

This next portion transitions away from the focus on the eternality of Jesus Christ toward his incarnation on earth. This marks the expressed condescension of Christ, as Philippians 2:6–8 notes, 'who, though he was in the form of God, did not count equality with God a thing to be grasped, but emptied himself, by taking the form of a servant, being made in the likeness of men. And being found in human form, he humbled himself by becoming obedient to the point of death, even death on a cross.' The eternal Son of God, the creed notes, 'came down from heaven and was incarnate by the Holy Spirit of the Virgin Mary, and was made man.' For what purpose? Why did the Son descend from heaven to visit His people on earth? He did so 'for us men and for our salvation.' Jesus came to save His people from their sins (Matt. 1:21; Mark 10:45;

John 3:16–17; 1 John 2:2; etc.). This was the truth that Arius and his followers were stumbling over. They affirmed the humanity of Jesus and His earthly ministry to God's people, yet they denied His divinity.

By the time of the Council of Constantinople in 381, however, a reactionary view arose through a man named Apollinaris of Laodicea. Contrary to Arius, Apollinaris espoused the view that Jesus Christ was truly divine but not truly human. While he taught that Christ did have a human body, he maintained that He did not have a human mind, since the human mind is the origin of all sinful thoughts. He reasoned that were Christ to have a human mind, He could not maintain sinlessness.

However, Gregory of Nazianzus responded with the argument: 'What has not been taken up has not been healed.' In other words, Christ could not come to redeem and save the sinfulness of the human mind if He Himself did not take up a human mind. Gregory continued, 'Once He [Christ] was not a man, but only God the Son, existing before all the ages, and He was not connected with a body or anything physical; but now He has become man too, taking humanity upon Himself for our salvation.'[13] Had Jesus not 'came down from heaven' and 'made man,' He would not have been able to act as our substitute on the cross, dying to pay the penalty of sinful men, and resurrecting again to new life 'for our salvation.' In the end, Apollinarianism was condemned at Constantinople.

And was crucified also for us under Pontius Pilate; he suffered and was buried; and the third day he rose again, according to the Scriptures;
This section of the creed reads similarly to the Apostles' Creed. It grounds the events of Jesus' crucifixion and death

---

13. Quoted in Nick Needham, *2000 Years of Christ's Power: The Age of the Early Church Fathers* (Fearn, Ross-shire: Christian Focus, 2016), 312.

in world history, effectively naming the Roman governor who presided over the epoch-changing event. Unlike the Apostles' Creed, Jesus' death is not specifically noted, but the fact that 'he suffered,' 'was crucified,' and 'was buried' lends itself to that logical conclusion. However, this section reflects the pattern of 1 Corinthians 15:3–4, where Paul notes 'that [Jesus] was raised on the third day according to the Scriptures.' Again, compared to the Apostles' Creed, this creed grounds the events of Jesus' death, burial, and resurrection in the authority of the Scriptures, further intensifying the veracity of the declaration.

And ascended into heaven, and sits on the right hand of the Father; and he shall come again, with glory, to judge the living and the dead; whose kingdom shall have no end.
This portion regarding Christ's ascension, return, and judgment are virtually identical to the verbiage of the Apostles' Creed, with the addition of a phrase taken from Luke 1:33, 'of his kingdom there will be no end.' While these phrases regarding Christ's ascension and return in judgment would otherwise seem to be standard fare for most creeds, they hold particular weight in this creed. Remember that the key theological debate was over the full divinity of the Son, which this creed sought to articulate.

However, these three realities—ascension, return, judgment—are notable features of Christ's deity. In his conversation with Nicodemus, Jesus declared, 'No one has ascended into heaven except he who descended from heaven, the Son of Man' (John 3:13). The statement speaks to the exclusivity of who is allowed to ascend and descend—certainly not mere humans! Were Jesus to be human only, as Arius claimed, he would not be permitted to ascend and descend.

Furthermore, divine judgment is an action reserved for God alone. Yet Jesus declares in John 5:22–23 that '[the Father] has given all judgment to the Son, that all may honor the Son, just as they honor the Father. Whoever does not honor the Son does not honor the Father who sent Him.' Frankly, this is a blasphemous statement if the Son of God is not truly divine, as God does not share his glory with anyone (Isa. 42:8), that is, unless it is with one who is God Himself.

And I believe in the Holy Spirit, the Lord and Giver of life; who proceeds from the Father and the Son;

The Creed of Nicaea only gives the Holy Spirit a single line: 'And [I believe] in the Holy Spirit.' While this articulation was sufficient in earlier creeds, the Council of Constantinople labored to fill out the doctrine of the Holy Spirit. By the late 350s Athanasius had begun to expound on his theology of the Spirit. However, the torch would be carried further by others after Athanasius' death. J.N.D. Kelly notes, 'If Athanasius took the lead in defending the homoousion of the Spirit, the task was completed, cautiously and circumspectly, by the Cappadocian fathers.'[14]

The creed calls the Spirit 'the Lord and Giver of life.' In many ways, this mirrors the designations given to the Son, as 'the *Lord* Jesus Christ' and the one 'by whom all things were made' (cf. John 1:3, 10; 1 Cor. 8:6; Col. 1:16; Heb. 1:2). This expression of the Spirit is meant to demonstrate His equality with the Father and the Son. In the Bible, while the title of 'Lord' is most frequently assigned to Jesus, there are passing references to the Spirit's lordship, such as 2 Corinthians 3:17: 'Now the Lord is the Spirit, and where the Spirit of the Lord is, there is freedom.' While not confusing the persons of the Son and the Spirit, it is appropriate to submit to the Spirit as 'Lord.' As for the Spirit being the 'Giver of life,' there are many biblical references to the life-giving power of the Holy Spirit (Job 33:4; Ezek. 37:14; John 6:63; Rom. 8:2, 6; 2 Cor. 3:6).

---

14. Kelly, *Early Christian Doctrines*, 258.

When seeking to defend the deity of the Spirit, the Cappadocian fathers employed a term that would be akin to expressing the relationship between the Father and the Son. Gregory of Nazianzus famously questioned, 'What then? Is the Spirit God? Most certainly. Well then, is he consubstantial [with the Father and the Son]? Yes, if he is God.'[15] But how was this to be expressed? If the Son is the *only-begotten* of the Father, they reasoned, then the Spirit could not also be regarded as being begotten also. Rather, they drew a connection expressed by Jesus in John 15:26: 'But when the Helper comes, whom I will send to you from the Father, the Spirit of truth, who *proceeds* from the Father, he will bear witness about me' (emphasis added). Therefore, they assert the declaration that the Spirit '*proceeds* from the Father and the Son.'[16] In this way, it functions as a parallel which places the Spirit on the same divine plane as the Son in the relation to the Father. How exactly is it that the Spirit proceeds from the Father and the Son? The early church fathers readily admitted that such knowledge belonged to the divine mystery.

Who with the Father and the Son together is worshiped and glorified; who spoke by the prophets.
Only a few years prior to the Council of Constantinople, Basil the Great published his work *On the Holy Spirit*, in which he argued for the full deity and consubstantiality of the Spirit. Seemingly inspired by Basil, the framers of the Nicene Creed inserted the affirmation that the Spirit is to be 'worshiped and glorified' along with the Father and the Son. This statement further intensifies the truth that the Father, the Son, and the Spirit are of the same essence (*homoousios*). They are all

---

15. Quoted in Allison, *Historical Theology*, 436.

16. Some early Greek versions of the creed express the Holy Spirit's procession from the Father only, but more universally accepted versions in the West express the connection both to the Father and the Son. This is known as the *Filioque*.

equally of the same divine substance. And because of this, they are fully and equally worthy of being worshiped and glorified as God. But how is the unity of the Godhead to be expressed without confusing or confounding them?

One of the challenges that arose in the wake of Nicaea was the confusion between the usage of two words: *ousia* and *hypostasis*. In the Greek language, the words are virtually synonymous, having to do with the 'substance,' or essence, and personhood of God.[17] The Cappadocian fathers reconciled this difference by using the word *ousia* to refer to the divine essence, of which the Father and Son (as well as the Spirit) partake fully and equally, making the three persons one God. When using the word *hypostasis*, however, they employed it to refer to the distinct form (personhood) in which the divine essence of the Father and the Son exists.[18] In this way, they were able to reconcile the biblical truth that there is but one God (one *ousia*) who exists eternally in three distinct persons (three *hypostases*).

The next phrase is the only indirect reference to the inspiration of Scripture in the Nicene Creed, and it applies to the ministry of the Spirit. The creed declares that he 'spoke by the prophets,' no doubt a reference to verses such as 2 Peter 1:20–21.[19] In this way, God the Spirit inspires the

---

17. Donald Fairbairn notes that some Eastern bishops were using *hypostasis* and *ousia* synonymously, while others rendered *hypostasis* to mean 'person.' Many of these church leaders were talking past one another, not able to arrive at an agreed upon usage of the words. This is why the contribution of the Cappadocian fathers was so significant. Donald Fairbairn and Ryan M. Reeves, *The Story of Creeds and Confessions: Tracing the Development of the Christian Faith* (Grand Rapids: Baker Academic, 2019), 68–69.

18. There is a helpful explanation of this distinction in Nick Needham, *2000 Years of Christ's Power: The Age of the Early Church Fathers* (Fearn, Ross-shire: Christian Focus, 2016), 238.

19. 'But know this first of all, that no prophecy of Scripture is a matter of one's own interpretation, for no prophecy was ever made by an act of human will, but men

revelation of His Word through the mouths of the prophets (cf. John 14:17, 26; 16:13; 2 Tim 3:16–17).

And I believe in one holy catholic and apostolic church.

This line is very similar to the Apostles' Creed yet with a few additions, namely 'one' and 'apostolic.' As mentioned in the previous chapter, the universal ('catholic') church of Jesus Christ is called to be 'holy'—set apart for his purposes. But the Nicene Creed's expression of the doctrine of the church adds two key aspects—its unity and authority.

As to its unity, the Scriptures speak of the spiritual oneness of the church (e.g. John 17:23; Gal. 3:28; Eph. 4:3, 13). Furthermore, early church fathers like Clement of Alexandria noted the distinguishing mark of oneness, writing, 'The preeminence of the church, as the principle of unity, is its oneness. In this, it surpasses all other things and has nothing like or equal to itself.'[20] The unity of believers within the church of Jesus Christ is meant to reflect the perfect unity within the Godhead, as we are redeemed by the will of the Father, through the work of the Son, according to ministry of the Spirit (Eph. 1:3–14).

Regarding the reference to the 'apostolic' church, the expression is meant to convey that all true Christian believers are together in fellowship with the foundational ministry of the apostles (cf. Acts 2:42–47; 1 Cor. 12:28; Eph. 2:20), which was appointed by none other than Jesus Christ Himself (Matt. 10:2–4; cf. 1 Cor. 9:1). This designation of fellowship with the 'apostolic' church is set over and against the rampant heretical teaching which arose in the years prior to the Council of Constantinople. By citing adherence to the 'one holy catholic and apostolic church,' the church fathers were grounding their

---

moved by the Holy Spirit spoke from God' (2 Pet. 1:20–21, NASB95).

20. Quoted in Allison, *Historical Theology*, 567.

doctrine in the authority of the ministry established by Jesus Christ through his appointed apostles.

I acknowledge one baptism for the remission of sins; and I look for the resurrection of the dead, and the life of the world to come. Amen.

Rooted in the united, sanctified, universal, and authoritative witness of the church given previously are a series of acknowledgements of core Christian doctrine. While the Apostles' Creed professes the belief in 'the forgiveness of sins,' the Nicene Creed makes reference to the 'one baptism for the remission of sins.' The Bible records Jesus' authoritative command to: 'Go therefore and make disciples of all the nations, *baptizing them* in the name of the Father and of the Son and of the Holy Spirit' (Matt. 28:19, emphasis added; cf. Acts 2:38). While the apostle Paul connects the believer's spiritual baptism to the sacrificial work of Jesus Christ on the cross (Rom. 6:3-4), the obedience of physical water baptism functions as an identifying marker that the believer has had their sins forgiven because of Christ's death, burial, and resurrection.

Similar to the language of the Apostles' Creed, we read the expressed hope of the believer for future realities, namely 'the resurrection of the dead and the life of the world to come.' Both of these realities are promised to those who belong to Jesus Christ (Rev. 20:4-6). In the end, it is only by saving faith in Jesus Christ that there is to be any future hope. And yet, to declare: 'I believe in one God, the Father Almighty...and in one Lord Jesus Christ, the only-begotten Son of God...and in the Holy Spirit, the Lord and Giver of life' is to profess faith in the only true God who is able to redeem that which has been lost. And in true creedal fashion, the declaration is sealed with a testimony of affirmation: 'Amen.'

4

The Definition of Chalcedon

The Nicene Creed was a triumphant success, effectively confessing the full deity of both the Son and the Spirit, along with the Father, to articulate an expression of Trinitarian theology. In the years following the finalization of the creed, a new question began to arise: how can Jesus Christ be at the same time God and man? The discussions and debates of the early fifth century eventually produced, what Chad Van Dixhoorn calls 'the clearest statement to date on the person of the Lord Jesus Christ'[1]—known as the Formula or Definition of Chalcedon.

BACKGROUND

While the Arian heresy was effectively squashed at both the Councils of Nicaea and Constantinople, its faulty reactionary movement, known as Apollinarianism, was still alive and being debated, despite being condemned in 381. At the same time, toward the end of the fourth century, two main schools of thought began to crystalize. The first theological group consisted of the theologians of Antioch (known as

---

1. Chad Van Dixhoorn, ed. *Creeds, Confessions, and Catechisms: A Reader's Edition* (Wheaton: Crossway, 2022), 25.

the 'Antiochenes'). The Antiochenes, which included church leaders such as Diodore of Tarsus, Theodore of Mopsuestia, and Nestorius, emphasized a more literalistic interpretation of the Scriptures. The second theological group, which comprised such leaders as Athanasius, Apollinaris, Cyril of Alexandria, and Eutyches, was known as the 'Alexandrians.' They emphasized a more allegorical reading of the Scriptures. Naturally, when the question arose about the mystery of the incarnation of Jesus Christ, both groups fiercely collided.

In their response to Apollinarianism—the view that Jesus Christ was fully God but not fully man—the Antiochenes lurched in the opposition direction. Whereas Apollinaris reasoned that Christ could not possess a truly human mind and yet be sinless, the Antiochenes sought to draw a stark distinction between Christ's two natures, thus attempting to preserve the integrity of both. However, one Antiochene preacher named Nestorius brought the distinction too far, espousing the view that there are essentially two distinct persons—the one human person of Jesus of Nazareth who was spiritually indwelt by the person of the divine *Logos* (the Greek rendering of the 'Word' in John 1:1–4, 14). In this way, Nestorius taught that Jesus was merely an especially graced human man with whom the divine Son of God had united Himself.[2] However, this is not how Scripture presents, or the church had understood, the incarnation of Jesus Christ.

The strongest reaction to the views of Nestorius came from Cyril of Alexandria. Serving as bishop of Alexandria from 412 until his death in 444, Cyril was a profound thinker and preeminent theologian. Despite his theological brilliance, however, Cyril was merciless toward his opponents, often seeking not only to destroy their arguments but also

---

2. This general phrasing is borrowed from Nick Needham's explanation of Nestorius' views in his book *2000 Years of Christ's Power: The Age of the Early Church Fathers* (Fearn, Ross-shire: Christian Focus, 2016), 298.

their reputations as well. When Nestorius' Christological positions became public, Cyril pounced on him, plunging the Antiochenes and Alexandrians into severe conflict. Yet despite the rampant disagreements between them, at certain points it almost seemed like both sides were talking past each other. Much of the confusion stemmed from the use of terminology. In discussing the nature and personhood of Jesus Christ, the Cappadocian fathers had employed the use of the words *ousia* (essence/substance) and *hypostasis* (person). However, by the time of Nestorius and Cyril, more terms were being considered. The word *physis* was being used to describe personal nature, while *prosōpon* was employed to talk about personhood.

Antiochenes such as Diodore and Theodore spoke of Christ as consisting of two *physeis* (two natures) and one *prosōpon* (one person).[3] However, Cyril understood Nestorius and company as teaching that there were two separate persons in Christ. In this way, he believed that the eternal Word (*Logos*) came down and indwelt the human person of Jesus, taking over his body. But Cyril rejected this position as wholly errant, reasoning that there was in fact a perfect *hypostatic union*—that 'the natures which are brought together into this true union are different, but out of the two there is one Christ, one Son, the difference of natures not being destroyed as a result of the union.'[4] While a debate still rages as to whether or not Nestorius actually believed and taught the existence of two Christs,[5] his name soon became synonymous with the Christological error and a firestorm ensued.

---

3. Donald Fairbairn and Ryan M. Reeves, *The Story of Creeds and Confessions: Tracing the Development of the Christian Faith* (Grand Rapids: Baker Academic, 2019), 81.

4. Quoted in J.N.D. Kelly, *Early Christian Doctrines*. Revised Edition (New York: HarperOne, 1978), 313.

5. One of the most helpful evaluations of Nestorius' theology and misrepresentation comes in J.N.D. Kelly, *Early Christian Doctrines*. Revised Edition (New York: HarperOne, 1978), 310–317.

By 430 Cyril had brought the matter as far as Pope Celestine who in turn called for a synod to be held in Rome later that year. The synod ruled that Nestorius was in the wrong, which resulted in Cyril penning a provocative document known as the Twelve Anathemas, summarizing each of Nestorius' errors. Both the synod and the document further fueled the growing fire which essentially turned into a battle of rival synods, each condemning the other side. Finally, Emperor Theodosius convened an ecumenical council at Ephesus in June 431 to attempt to settle the doctrinal dispute. While the council favored Cyril, deposing Nestorius, tensions between the two sides were at an all-time high.

After two more years of contentious fighting between the Antiochenes and Alexandrians, a consorted effort was made to heal the dispute. Two of the key figures aimed at brokering peace were Cyril of Alexandria and a bishop named John of Antioch. Fully convinced that the Antiochenes were being misunderstood and misrepresented, John corresponded with Cyril to attempt to reconcile their theological rift. The result was a document known as the Formula of Union (433). Contained in the brief joint statement was the following:

> We confess, therefore, our Lord Jesus Christ, the only-begotten Son of God, perfect God and perfect man composed of a rational soul and a body, begotten before the ages from His Father in respect of His divinity, but likewise in these last days for us and for our salvation from the Virgin Mary in respect of His manhood, consubstantial with the Father in respect of His divinity and at the same time consubstantial with us in respect of His manhood. For a union of two natures has been accomplished. Hence we confess one Christ, one Son, one Lord.[6]

---

6.   Quoted in Kelly, *Early Christian Doctrines*, 328–329.

Despite Nestorius' continued condemnation, orthodoxy had been successfully and agreeably upheld, and a temporary peace was secured. But it would not last.

After the deaths of John (in 441) and Cyril (in 444), a new controversy emerged involving an aging archimandrite teacher named Eutyches. A follower of Cyril's theology, Eutyches taught an extreme version of the hypostatic union that was, in fact, so united that the two natures (*physeis*) of Jesus Christ merged, with the divine nature swallowing up the human nature. This would eventually become known as the Monophysite heresy (also known as Eutychianism). Before too long, Eutyches was denounced by a synod in Constantinople and formally condemned by Flavian, the patriarch of the city in 448. One year later Pope Leo wrote a letter to Flavian, later known as his *Tome*, addressing Eutyches' errors and reaffirming Christological orthodoxy. One of his powerful allies, Dioscorus, the new patriarch of Alexandria, was furious at Eutyches' condemnation, and called for Emperor Theodosius to summon a new council at Ephesus in 449. What came to be known as the Second Council of Ephesus effectively rolled back the theological progress of the previous twenty years, earning it the nickname, 'The Robber Synod.'

After the untimely death of Theodosius, the new emperor, Marcian, summoned an ecumenical council to meet in Chalcedon in 451 to settle the Christological disputes and re-establish orthodoxy. The council commenced on October 8, 451 with more than five hundred bishops attending from all over the empire. The council read aloud and reaffirmed the Nicene Creed, as well as the Christological doctrine laid out in Pope Leo's *Tome* and the writings of Cyril of Alexandria. In addition, they evaluated the theologies of Nestorius and Eutyches, ultimately ruling them as errant. In order to bridge the divide that had existed between the Antiochenes and Alexandrians, the emperor wanted the council to draft a new creed, but the majority of bishops were against it. They agreed instead to compose a 'definition' that would further explain Nicaea's doctrine of Christ. While the final document consisted of several pages, there was one succinct paragraph about the Son of God, which is now known as the Definition of Chalcedon. In addition to the new definition, the council reversed all of the rulings of the 'Robber Synod' two years prior, as well as deposed Dioscorus of Alexandria. In the end, the Council of Chalcedon succeeded in affirming the doctrinal work done at the first three ecumenical councils of Nicaea, Constantinople, and Ephesus, thus solidifying Christological orthodoxy for all posterity.

THE DEFINITION OF CHALCEDON

The Definition of Chalcedon consists of two main parts. The first part essentially restates the key theological declarations from the Nicene Creed, while the second part summarizes the theological consensus surrounding the events of both Councils of Ephesus (431) and Chalcedon (451).[7] Philip Schaff notes that the definition 'indicates the essential elements of Christological truth, and the boundary-lines of Christological error.'[8] What are these boundaries? Carl Trueman expresses them:

[1.] Christ must be fully God; [2.] Christ must be fully human: [3.] the two natures must not be so mixed together that either disappears into the other or that a third, hybrid nature is produced; [4.] and the two natures must not be separated so as to undermine the unity of the one person.[9]

---

7. J.N.D. Kelly notes that, in addition to affirming the doctrine of Nicaea and Constantinople, the final version of the statement included excerpts from Cyril's two Letters, Pope Leo's *Tome*, the Union Symbol [the Formula of Union] and Flavian's profession of faith at the Standing Synod. *Early Christian Doctrines*. Revised Edition (New York: HarperOne, 1978), 340–341.

8. Philip Schaff, *The Creeds of Christendom* (1931; republished, Grand Rapids: Baker Books, 2007), I:34.

9. Carl R. Trueman, *The Creedal Imperative* (Wheaton: Crossway, 2012), 100.

Expertly establishing these Christological bounds, the definition consists of the following:

Following the saintly fathers, we all with one voice teach the confession of one and the same Son, our Lord Jesus Christ:
The bishops at the Council of Chalcedon were keenly aware that they were standing on the shoulders of their 'saintly fathers,' namely men like Alexander, Athanasius, the Cappadocian fathers, and Cyril of Alexandria. Furthermore, the definition merged the core Christological doctrines of both the Antiochenes and Alexandrians in a way that they could all affirm together: 'We all with one voice teach the confession.'

To satisfy the concerns of the Alexandrians, the council affirmed, 'one and the same Son, our Lord Jesus Christ.' This was over and against the issues raised against Nestorius, that there was such a divide in the Lord so as to produce *two Sons* or *two Christs*. So emphatic were the framers of the statement that they repeated the phrase 'one and the same' three times, each referring to a different aspect of the Christological doctrine, with each re-statement of 'one and the same' increasing in specificity.

The same perfect in divinity and perfect in humanity, the same truly God and truly man, of a rational soul and a body; consubstantial with the Father as regards his divinity, and the same consubstantial with us as regards his humanity; like us in all respects except for sin;
The word 'same' is repeated five times in the brief definition, the first of them occurring here. This *same*-ness emphasizes Christ's being of one substance with the Father, as well as of one substance with humanity. Not at all less than God or less than humanity, the statement affirms that Jesus is 'perfect in divinity and perfect in humanity.' In further clarifying the sentiment, we read 'the same truly God and truly man.' Whereas every heresy

up to that point had diminished either the deity or humanity of Jesus Christ, the bishops at Chalcedon declared boldly that He is at the same time 'truly God' in all his fullness (Col. 1:19, 2:9; Heb. 1:3), and 'truly man,' to which the statement adds, 'rational soul and a body'—a statement reflecting His true humanity (Phil. 2:7; Heb. 2:17).

The next phrase restates the key assertion from Nicaea, namely that the Son is 'consubstantial with the Father as regards his divinity.' This was the main issue for the bishops contending for the truth against the Arians who denied the deity of Jesus Christ. The definition uses the same word featured as before— *homoousios* (of the same substance, or essence). However, the bishops at Chalcedon also added that Christ was 'consubstantial [*homoousios*] with us as regards his humanity.' As the incarnate Son, Jesus is not somehow less than human, nor is he super-human. He is of the same human substance with us, yet with one exception—he is 'like us in all respects except for sin.' This key tenet of Christian orthodoxy is rooted in such verses as 2 Corinthians 5:21, Hebrews 4:15, 7:26, and 1 Peter 2:21–22. In order for Jesus Christ to pay for sins as an acceptable sacrifice, He must Himself be without sin. Furthermore, were Jesus to be guilty of sin, it would impugn his divine character as God.

Begotten before the ages from the Father as regards his divinity, and in the last days the same for us and for our salvation from Mary, the virgin God-bearer, as regards his humanity;
The next phrase reflects not only a staple of Nicene orthodoxy but also a core biblical truth—the declaration that the Son of God is 'begotten before the ages from the Father.' Arius had claimed that the Son was created by God, begotten in time. However, the opening verses of John 1 clearly testify to the fact that the Son was *already* 'in the beginning with

God' (John 1:2). Yet the Bible refers to the Son as being 'only-begotten' (*monogenes*) of the Father (John 1:14, 18; 3:16, 18; Heb. 1:5; 1 John 4:9; etc.). Theologians refer to this concept as the *eternal generation* of the Son, meaning that, while the Son is begotten from the Father, He is begotten eternally, and therefore has no beginning. This eternality is expressed by the phrase 'before the ages.' Jesus has always been truly God, of the same divine substance as the Father.

Perhaps the first hint of trouble for Nestorius was his public rejection of the designation of the virgin Mary as the *theotokos* ('God-bearer'). While he did not deny the virgin birth itself, he was uncomfortable with the notion that the eternal God of creation had a mother. He had offered an alternate term—*christotokos* ('Christ-bearer'). However, the term *theotokos* would later become standard orthodoxy, not that Mary was somehow the mother of eternal deity, but that for the incarnation of Jesus Christ to be true, His two natures must unite in the womb of His earthly mother. Cyril noted,

> The holy fathers...ventured to call the holy virgin the Mother of God [*theotokos*: God bearer], not as if the nature of the Word of his divinity had its beginning from the holy virgin, but because of her was born that holy body with a rational soul, to which the Word being personally united is said to be born according to the flesh.[10]

The concept of Mary being the 'mother of God' may seem odd to Protestant ears, but as the Alexandrians reasoned, if Jesus Christ is God, and Mary gave birth to Christ, then He who was born of her was God.[11]

---

10. Quoted in Gregg R. Allison, *Historical Theology: An Introduction to Christian Doctrine* (Grand Rapids: Zondervan, 2011), 374.

11. Needham, *2000 Years of Christ's Power*, 297.

one and the same Christ, Son, Lord, only-begotten,

This second occurrence of 'one and the same' expands the first instance—that Jesus is 'one and the same Christ, Son, Lord only-begotten.' This phrase voices the concern of the Alexandrians, that there are not somehow two divided persons—the 'Christ' and the 'Son,' or the 'Lord' and the 'only-begotten' Son of God. These titles do not refer to separate persons. As Donald Fairbairn maintains, '[Christ] is the same one who has always been God's Only-begotten.'[12]

Acknowledged in two natures which undergo no confusion, no change, no division, no separation;

This portion of the statement gets to the heart of the matter. This is where both Alexandrians and Antiochenes sought to find common ground regarding the burning question about the true identity of Jesus Christ. How is it possible that Jesus Christ is at the same time 'truly God and truly man'? Had Cyril been alive and present at Chalcedon he no doubt would have argued strenuously for the phrase *hypostatic union*, as it conveys the core of orthodox Christology. Nevertheless, its truth is clearly articulated.

Up to this point, the statement has been zeroing in on the two natures of Christ and how they are related. Concerned about Eutyches' merging of the two natures of Christ into one, the council rejected his wording '*from* two natures' and embraced the more distinct affirmation, '*in* two natures.' In a slight departure from the language of Nicaea, Christ's two natures are referred to as two *physeis*, which the bishops closely aligned with the word *ousia* (essence/nature/substance). This is the way that Christ can be 'perfect in divinity,' being of the same divine nature as the Father, and also 'perfect in humanity,' being of the same human nature as us—two complete natures.

---

12. Fairbairn and Reeves, *The Story of Creeds and Confessions*, 103.

But how are these natures related? This was a great challenge for them. Instead of trying to articulate an exact metaphysical understanding of the relationship between Christ's two natures, the bishops opted instead to deal in *apophatic*, or 'negative,' theological language. They believed that the best way to articulate the truth of Christ was to declare what was definitively *not* true about Him. Harry Boer notes, 'The wisdom of Chalcedon is that it did not attempt to say *how* the natures are united in Christ. Rather, it warned against how they are *not* united.'[13]

Four negatives are listed out, comprising two distinct pairs. The first pair listed refers to the fact that with regard to Christ's two natures, there is 'no confusion, no change.' These two terms addressed the Antiochenes concerns about the Alexandrian tendency to unite the natures into one or confuse them, as was the error of Eutyches. Christ's divine nature and human nature remain perfect, with no chance of corruption or amalgamation.

The second pair address the Antiochene tendency to divide or separate Christ's natures, as was the case with Nestorius. To answer this error, the bishops declared that there is 'no division, no separation' of his natures. To turn a modern phrase, Christ doesn't suffer from a multiple personality disorder. He is not divided against Himself. Rather His two natures—divine and human—are united together perfectly.

At no point was the difference between the two natures taken away through the union, but rather the property of both natures is preserved and comes together into a single person and a single subsistent being;

In further explaining the union of Christ's two natures, the definition adds, 'at no point was the difference between

13. Harry R. Boer, *A Short History of the Early Church* (Grand Rapids: Eerdmans, 1976), 171–172.

natures taken away through the union.' The Lord did not lose anything by becoming incarnate and taking on a human body. When Philippians 2:7 speaks of Christ '[emptying] himself, by taking the form of a servant, being born in the likeness of men,' we understand that He did not surrender even one fragment of his deity. 'But rather,' the bishops recognized, 'the property of both natures is preserved.' Earlier Cyril had written, 'The natures which are brought together into this true union are different, but out of the two there is one Christ, one Son, the difference of natures not being destroyed as a result of the union.'[14]

However, what is produced in the uniting of these two natures? The statement affirms not the existence of two persons, as the Nestorians claimed, but rather that 'the property of both natures...comes together into a single person [*prosōpon*] and a single subsistent [*hypostasis*] being.' The bishops associated both words *hypostasis* and *prosōpon* with the notion of a 'person.' In other words, there is not a divine Jesus Christ and a human Jesus Christ; there is *one* Jesus Christ who embodies two distinct yet united natures.

He is not parted or divided into two persons, but is one and the same only-begotten Son, God, Word, Lord Jesus Christ,
Restated another way, the definition further clarifies that Jesus Christ 'is not parted or divided into two persons,' again putting one final nail in the coffin of Nestorianism. Combined with the previous *apophatic* affirmation of 'no division, no separation,' the union of Christ's two natures is upheld. And the expression of the *two-natures-in-one-person* reality established the orthodox position of Jesus Christ as the 'God-man.'

In the third and final expression of the 'one and the same' phrases of the statement, the bishops articulated definitively that Jesus 'is one and the same only-begotten Son,

---

14. Quoted in Kelly, *Early Christian Doctrines*, 313.

God, Word, Lord Jesus Christ.' As the 'only-begotten Son' He is 'one and the same' essence with the Father. As the 'Word' (John 1:1–3, 14), He is 'one and the same' God—*truly* God. As the 'Lord Jesus Christ' He is 'one and the same,' and not the composition, for example, of a *human* Jesus and a *divine* Christ. He is the one and only Lord Jesus Christ.

Just as the prophets taught from the beginning about him, and as the Lord Jesus Christ himself instructed us, and as the creed of the fathers handed it down to us.
In the closing of the definition, the bishops testify to the fact that their doctrinal pursuits were not the product of their own invention. They were not simply creating some new doctrine of Christ. And in this final statement, they affirm three sources from which they derived their doctrine. First, they acknowledge 'the prophets [who] taught from the beginning about him.' This is no less than the written testimony of Scripture, both Old and New Testaments. They were relying on such glorious Christological passages like John 1:1–18, Philippians 2:5–11, Colossians 1:15–20, and others, as well as the many passages in Hebrews.

Furthermore, they meticulously studied the self-revelation of Jesus Christ in the Gospels. In many places Jesus claimed equality with the Father—e.g. 'Believe me that I am in the Father and the Father is in me' (John 14:11), 'I and the Father are one' (John 10:30). He also claimed to be the unique agent of the Father—e.g. 'I can do nothing on my own. As I hear, I judge, and my judgment is just, because I seek not my own will but the will of him who sent Me' (John 5:30), 'I have come in My Father's name, and you do not receive me' (John 5:43), 'No one can come to me unless the Father who sent me draws him. And I will raise him up on the last day' (John 6:44). Even beyond His unbreakable union with God the Father, Jesus claims the very name of God Himself: 'Truly, Truly, I say to you, before Abraham was, *I am*' (John 8:58).

Lastly, the bishops at Chalcedon adhered to the teaching 'as the creed of the fathers handed it down to us.' This is no doubt the Nicene Creed, as well as the theological writings surrounding it. Again, the purpose of the Council of Chalcedon was not to write a new creed but to explain the Christological doctrine expressed in the Nicene Creed. While the Definition of Chalcedon did not answer all of the questions that could be asked, it succeeded in establishing the baseline of Christological orthodoxy for their own generation, and for every Christian generation that was to come.

5

The Athanasian Creed

The timeless question persists: *What is the minimum standard of orthodoxy that must be believed in order to be considered a Christian?* Various answers have been offered. However, one widely accepted statement consisting of forty-four verses has claimed the title; if ever there were such a title, 'Definitive Test of Essential Orthodoxy,' it would belong to the Athanasian Creed, and this distinction would not be unfounded. Martin Luther deemed it to be 'the most important and glorious composition since the days of the apostles.'[1] The creed has been in regular usage for more than fifteen-hundred years and has found approval in the Augsburg Confession, the Form of Concord, the Thirty-nine Articles, and the Second Helvetic Confession. In short, the Athanasian Creed has stood the test of time as a symbol of Christian orthodoxy.

BACKGROUND

The origin of the doctrinal statement known as The Athanasian Creed is unknown. Scholar J.N.D. Kelly notes, 'the only two assured facts about the Athanasian Creed are that it is neither

---

1. Philip Schaff, *The Creeds of Christendom* (1931; republished, Grand Rapids: Baker Books, 2007), I:41.

a creed nor by Athanasius.'[2] Not discouraged by this maxim, Donald Fairbairn refers to it as 'a creedal anomaly with staying power.'[3] However uncertain its origins, what we now universally refer to as the Athanasian Creed is well-loved and widely accepted as a standard of Christian orthodoxy in many corners of the world.

As early as the ninth century, Athanasius of Alexandria had been credited with writing the creed. For centuries the creed went by many names including 'The Faith of Athanasius' and 'The Catholic Faith,' even 'The Catholic Faith of St. Athanasius.' However, by the seventeenth century, both Roman Catholics and Protestants began to reject the theory of Athanasius as the author of the creed ascribed to him. The reasons for this are several.[4] First, the earliest manuscripts of the creed were written in Latin, not in Greek, which would have been Athanasius' primary language. Secondly, there is no reference made to the creed in any of Athanasius' own writings, or the writings of his contemporaries. Thirdly, the theology represented in the creed is most certainly post-Athanasian, even post-Nicaea; it reflects much of the work done by the Council of Constantinople in 381. Yet the fact that the creed bears his name functions more as an homage to 'the father of Nicene orthodoxy'—the bishop who spent his life contending for the essential truths of the Christian faith.

But who wrote the creed? Many theories have been put forward through the years. Based on the theology, writing style, and parallel quotations in the creed, several writers have been proposed such as Ambrose of Milan (339–397), Augustine of Hippo (354–430), Hilary of Arles (403–449),

---

2.   J.N.D. Kelly, *The Athanasian Creed* (New York: Harper & Row, 1964), 1.

3.   Donald Fairbairn and Ryan M. Reeves, *The Story of Creeds and Confessions: Tracing the Development of the Christian Faith* (Grand Rapids: Baker Academic, 2019), 126.

4.   Kelly, *The Athanasian Creed*, 2–3.

and Vincent of Lérins (d. 445). While no definitive solution has been reached, a large number of scholars believe that the creed was written sometime between 416 (after the publication of Augustine's *On the Trinity*) and 542 (the end of Caesarius of Arles' episcopate, in whose work the first reference was made).[5]

As for the content, Philip Schaff notes that the creed is 'a remarkably clear and precise summary of the doctrinal decisions of the first four ecumenical Councils (from 325 to 451), and the Augustinian speculations on the Trinity and the Incarnation.'[6] While not ever officially recognized by any ecumenical council, the Athanasian Creed has been used as a template for aspiring clergy for the purpose of mastering the essential doctrines of Christianity.[7]

THE ATHANASIAN CREED

The creed consists of two key parts. The first part (lines 3–28) lays out the basics of the doctrine of the Trinity. Lines 8 through 18 are clearly inspired (if not quoted verbatim) by Augustine's classic work *On the Trinity* (*De trinitate*). The second part (lines 29–43) expresses a summary of Chalcedonian Christology. Punctuating the creed (lines 1–2 and 44) are several 'damnatory' clauses that warn of the dangers of rejecting Christian orthodoxy.

[1] Whoever desires to be saved should above all hold to the catholic faith. [2] Anyone who does not keep it whole and unbroken will doubtless perish eternally.

In a notable departure from the earlier creeds, the Athanasian Creed begins with a series of warnings, or 'anathemas.' At first glance, these warnings appear jarring or even off-putting. However, Scripture often speaks in similar terms. For example,

---

5. Fairbairn and Reeves, *The Story of Creeds and Confessions*, 128.

6. Schaff, *The Creeds of Christendom*, I:37.

7. Fairbairn and Reeves, *The Story of Creeds and Confessions*, 129.

Jude 3 appeals to believers to 'contend for the faith that was once for all delivered to the saints.' Following that charge, he lays out a litany of severe warnings toward those who would corrupt Christian teaching, noting that they are 'designated for this condemnation' (v. 4), 'waterless clouds, swept along by winds; fruitless trees in late autumn, twice dead, uprooted; wild waves of the sea, casting up the foam of their own shame; wandering stars, for whom the gloom of utter darkness has been reserved forever' (v. 12–13), and so on. Furthermore, severe warnings against doctrinal corruption are prevalent throughout the epistles of Galatians, 2 Thessalonians, 1 and 2 Timothy, Titus, and 2 Peter.

More than this, Scripture testifies to the integral connection between knowledge and saving faith. In his prayer to the Father, Jesus confessed: 'And this is eternal life, that they know you, the only true God, and Jesus Christ whom you have sent' (John 17:3). In other words, the everlasting life of salvation is based on a doctrinally informed faith in God. You simply cannot believe in whom you do not know. In His jaw-dropping reply to the Pharisees, Jesus rebukes them for their lack of faith—specifically their faithless denial in Christ's deity—when He declared, 'I told you that you would die in your sins, for unless you believe that I am he [God] you will die in your sins' (John 8:24). Furthermore, we read the recorded sentiments of Jesus in Mark 16:16, 'Whoever believes and is baptized will be saved, but whoever does not believe will be condemned.' And while it must be said that mere mental assent to doctrinal facts does not save, true saving faith must be based on what God has revealed to us through His Word.

This is why the creed begins by asserting, 'Whoever desires to be saved should above all hold to the catholic faith.' As we saw earlier, the word 'catholic' does not mean Roman Catholic, as that distinction did not exist until five hundred years later.

What is meant by 'catholic' is *universal*. In other words, this is Christian doctrine that is believed and embraced by the whole professing church universal. Yet there are those who, as 1 John 2:19 testifies, 'went out from us, but they were not of us.' In doing so, they reject the gospel and 'turn away from listening to the truth and wander off into myths' (2 Tim. 4:4). And so, following the trajectory of Scripture, the creed acknowledges: 'Anyone who does not keep it [the faith] whole and unbroken will doubtless perish eternally.' False converts will always invariably deny the core tenets of Christianity as they fall away from it. But what is essential Christian faith?

[3] Now this is the catholic faith: that we worship one God in Trinity and the Trinity in unity, [4] neither confounding their persons nor dividing the essence. [5] For the person of the Father is a distinct person, the person of the Son is another, and that of the Holy Spirit still another. [6] But the divinity of the Father, Son, and Holy Spirit is one, the glory equal, the majesty coeternal.

After warning against rejecting 'the catholic faith,' the creed proceeds to identify what that universal Christian faith actually is. In previous creeds, the key imperative was to 'believe' certain truths about God, but this creed leads off with the affirmation that 'we *worship* one God in Trinity and the Trinity in unity.' It is at this point that this word *Trinity* is introduced. While the concept of 'the divine Triad' had been written about as early as the second century, it was the third-century bishop Tertullian who is credited with coining the term 'Trinity' to refer to the three persons of the Godhead.[8]

Here the mystery of the Trinity is put forth. In its brilliant and beautiful prose, the creed expresses the concept of

---

8.   J.N.D. Kelly, *Early Christian Doctrines*. Revised Edition (New York: HarperOne, 1978), 102, 110–115.

'one God in Trinity and the Trinity in unity.' This becomes the key sentiment that will steer the course of lines 3 through 28. As explored in previous creeds, this sentiment holds the paradox in tension—that God exists eternally in three distinct persons ('God in Trinity') and yet the Godhead is one indivisible essence ('Trinity in unity'). In safeguarding the statement, the creed sets the boundaries of orthodoxy against a multitude of condemned heresies—'neither confounding their persons' (as opposed to Monophysitism, for example) 'nor dividing the essence' (as opposed to Nestorianism).

The creed then outlines the parameters of the paradoxical tension by distinguishing between the members of the Trinity. First, we see the distinctiveness of each divine person: 'For the person of the Father is a distinct person, the person of the Son is another, and that of the Holy Spirit still another.' This sentence gives voice to the sentiment, 'one God in Trinity.' Yet in their distinctiveness, it is maintained that each member of the Trinity possesses the same glory and majesty as the other two.[9] We read: 'But the divinity of the Father, Son, and Holy Spirit is one, the glory equal, the majesty coeternal.' Their distinctiveness in no way harms or diminishes their shared divine glory. The emphatic nature of the first part of the creed stands in stark opposition to the early third-century heresy popularized by a Roman teacher named Sabellius known as *modalism*—the view that each member of the Trinity (Father, Son, and Spirit) are merely various modes or manifestations of one God.[10] The Athanasian Creed, however, refutes the lingering heresy.

---

9. Kelly, *The Athanasian Creed*, 74.

10. *Modalism*, often referred to as *Sabellianism*, is more specifically understood as *Modalistic Monarchianism*. The essence of the view is that God the Father manifested Himself as different modes at different times. This meant that the Father became the Son while on earth, who then died and rose again, and then manifested Himself as the Holy Spirit after His ascension.

[7] Such as the Father is, such is the Son and such is the Holy Spirit. [8] The Father is uncreated, the Son is uncreated, the Holy Spirit is uncreated. [9] The Father is immeasurable, the Son is immeasurable, the Holy Spirit is immeasurable. [10] The Father is eternal, the Son is eternal, the Holy Spirit is eternal. [11] And yet there are not three eternal beings; there is but one eternal being. [12] So too there are not three uncreated or immeasurable beings; there is but one uncreated and immeasurable being. [13] Similarly, the Father is almighty, the Son is almighty, the Holy Spirit is almighty. [14] Yet there are not three almighty beings; there is but one almighty being.

Building on the unity and oneness of the Trinity, these next lines of the creed take great pains to articulate divine attributes of each member of the Godhead. What is true and essential of one member of the Trinity is true for all the members: 'Such as the Father is, such is the Son and such is the Holy Spirit.' The creed then names several distinct attributes of God belonging to each person of the Trinity. Each is uncreated, immeasurable, eternal, and almighty. Not one of them is more or less than the other; these belong to all perfectly in unity.

In asserting the distinctiveness and completeness of each member of the Trinity, however, the creed is careful to avoid *Tritheism*—the belief that there are three gods. We read, 'And yet there are not three eternal beings; there is but one eternal being. So too there are not three uncreated or immeasurable beings; there is but one uncreated and immeasurable being.' This discussion of 'being' is important because it articulates Scripture's teaching in monotheism—'God is one' (Deut. 6:4; John 10:30; 1 Cor. 8:4; Eph. 4:6). God is 'one almighty being' who exists in three persons: Father, Son, and Holy Spirit.

[15] Thus, the Father is God, the Son is God, the Holy Spirit is God. [16] Yet there are not three gods; there is but one God. [17] Thus, the Father is Lord, the Son is Lord, the Holy Spirit is Lord. [18] Yet there are not three lords; there is but one Lord. [19] Just as Christian truth compels us to confess each person individually as both God and Lord, [20] so catholic religion forbids us to say that there are three gods or lords.

This portion of the creed asserts a core Christian truth: 'Thus, the Father is God, the Son is God, the Holy Spirit is God.' The divinity of each of the members of the Trinity is essential to the faith. In Exodus 3 Moses encounters God in the midst of the burning bush and asks Him to share His name. God responds, 'I AM WHO I AM' (Exod. 3:14). The English transliteration of the Hebrew letters amounts to YHWH, often pronounced, 'Yahweh' or 'Jehovah.' But of all the names and titles given for God in the Bible, we understand that the first divine person of the Trinity is known as God the Father (Matt. 6:9; 1 Cor. 8:6; Eph. 4:6; etc.). Based on the biblical evidence, the creed affirms 'the Father is God.'

The designation 'Son of God' is a messianic title (Ps. 2:7; Matt. 26:63; John 11:27; Heb. 1:5), but is more aptly understood as a divine title for the second person of the Trinity. Throughout the whole New Testament Jesus of Nazareth is referred to as 'the Son of God' (Matt. 8:29; 27:54; John 3:18; Acts 9:20; etc.) and 'the Son of Man' (Matt. 8:20; 9:6; 12:8; Mark 10:45; Luke 9:22; etc.). While the title of 'Son' denotes a specific relationship to the Father, as we will see, it no less refers to the absolute divinity of Jesus Christ. Countless verses in Scripture attest to Christ's divinity, such as Mark 2:5–7, John 1:1–3, 8:58, 17:5, 20:28, Philippians 2:6–11, Colossians 1:15–18, 2:9, Titus 2:13, Revelation 1:8, and more. In fact, as we have seen, the first four ecumenical councils rose in fierce opposition to those who challenged Christ's deity. In affirmation of His deity, the creed declares: 'the Son is God.'

Unfortunately, the Holy Spirit has suffered quite a bit through the course of church history from those who quickly dismissed His full deity and place within the Godhead. The Scriptures are replete with explicit references to His divinity (e.g. Matt. 12:31–32; Acts 5:3–4; 1 Cor. 2:10–11; 3:16; cf. Gen. 1:2; Titus 3:5; 2 Pet. 1:21), yet many in early church history diminished His deity and equality with the Father and the Son. In the mid-350s Athanasius began to expound on his own theology of the Spirit, while the Cappadocian fathers labored to crystalize his teaching into the collective consciousness of Christianity, with Basil of Caesarea penning the influential treatise, *On the Holy Spirit* in 375. The combined testimony of Scripture and historical theology resulted in the affirmation: 'the Holy Spirit is God.'

As lines 16 and 18 distinguish, there are not 'three gods' or 'three lords,' contrasting the heretical view of Tritheism. Rather the creed declares: 'Just as Christian truth compels us to confess each person individually as both God and Lord, so catholic religion forbids us to say that there are three gods or lords.' The thrust of this section is to declare the full and perfect unity of the Trinity.

[21] The Father was neither made nor created nor begotten from anyone. [22] The Son was neither made nor created; he was begotten from the Father alone. [23] The Holy Spirit was neither made nor created nor begotten; he proceeds from the Father and the Son. [24] Accordingly, there is one Father, not three fathers; there is one Son, not three sons; there is one Holy Spirit, not three holy spirits.

Up to this point, the creed has gone to great lengths to establish the unity of the persons of the Trinity. However, if their essence and being is identical, how then are they at all distinct? Lines 21 through 24 explain this. While each of the members of the Trinity are coequal and consubstantial, there exists eternal relationships between the members which are explored. What is often referred to as *modes of subsistence* is also known as 'eternal relations of origin.' It refers to 'the unique way the divine essence subsists (exists) in each person.'[11] How do they relate to one another?

The Scriptures affirm that the Father is infinite and eternal (e.g. Ps. 90:2; Isa. 40:28; Hab. 1:12; etc.), and therefore 'neither made nor created nor begotten from anyone.' In His infinitude and eternality, we understand that God is self-existent (known as His *aseity*). He has no origin; no one created, produced, or generated Him. Regarding His eternal relation to the other members, scholars refer to the Father's distinct property as *paternity*.

Like the Father, 'the Son was neither made nor created,' but the creed delineates what Scripture teaches—that the Son 'was begotten from the Father alone' (John 1:14, 18; 3:16, 18; Heb. 1:5; 5:5; 1 John 4:9). As discussed previously, the notion of the Son being 'begotten' refers to His eternal relationship to the Father. We only tend to understand the concept of a person being 'begotten' in time (everyone has a birthday!), but the notion that the Son of God is 'begotten from the Father' eternally pertains to the Son's consubstantial relation to the Father. J.N.D. Kelly notes that 'the Son derives His being from the Father alone, not by creation but by generation.'[12] Scholars refer to this as *filiation*.

Like with the Father and the Son, 'The Holy Spirit was neither made nor created'—He is coeternal and consubstantial—

---

11. Matthew Barrett, *Simply Trinity: The Unmanipulated Father, Son, and Spirit* (Grand Rapids: Baker Books, 2021), 322.

12. Kelly, *The Athanasian Creed*, 75.

but unlike the Son, He is not 'begotten.' The Bible portrays a different eternal relationship to the other members of the Trinity. Drawn from John 15:26, we understand that 'the Spirit of truth...*proceeds* from the Father (emphasis added).' The Spirit is not a second son of the Father, but in what is known as *procession* or *spiration*, He proceeds both from the Father, as well as the Son. This phrase, 'from the Father and the Son,' is known as the *Filioque* (sounds like 'Philly Oak Way') and refers to the affirmation that the Spirit is not only from the Father, but from the Son as well—something that was debated in earlier years but accepted in the West by the beginning of the fifth century.

Line 24 doubles down on the distinctiveness of each member of the Trinity: 'Accordingly, there is one Father, not three fathers; there is one Son, not three sons; there is one Holy Spirit, not three holy spirits.' Once again, this flies in the face of the modalistic heresy that somehow the Father becomes the Son who becomes the Spirit. Such confusion would undermine their eternal relationships and create an amalgamated Trinity in which the members blend into each other—a concept completely foreign to Scripture and church history.

[25] None in this Trinity is before or after, none is greater or smaller; [26] in their entirety the three persons are coeternal and coequal with each other. [27] So in everything, as was said earlier, the unity in Trinity, and the Trinity in unity, is to be worshiped. [28] Anyone then who desires to be saved should think thus about the Trinity.

The purpose of this opening section has been to articulate the orthodox understanding of the Trinity. While critics of the creeds and historical confessions often balk at the notion of the *Trinity*, citing that the word itself is foreign to the Bible, the doctrine of the Triune God is readily expressed in the

Scriptures. In the closing of Matthew's Gospel, for example, Jesus commands His disciples to 'make disciples of all the nations, baptizing them *in the name of the Father and of the Son and of the Holy Spirit*' (28:19, emphasis added). Here Jesus expresses all three persons equally, which the creed reflects: 'None in this Trinity is before or after, none is greater or smaller; in their entirety the three persons are coeternal and coequal with each other.'

And while it has been restated several times throughout the creed, the grand idea is that of 'the unity in Trinity, and the Trinity in unity.' Understanding this divine truth becomes the basis of our worship of the Triune God. Regarding such worship, we see the apostle Paul's closing benediction at the end of his second letter to the Corinthians which exults: 'The grace of the Lord Jesus Christ and the love of God and the fellowship of the Holy Spirit be with you all' (2 Cor. 13:14). While his purpose was not to enter into a theological study of the virtues that were to be associated with each member, Paul offers up a final word of praise to the Triune God.

In the closing line of this section, the creed issues somewhat of a softened warning about the importance of a right understanding of the Triune God. Line 28 asserts, 'Anyone then who desires to be saved should think thus about the Trinity.' As stated previously, it is not that possessing correct theology saves a person from the penalty of their sins. But true, saving faith is built on a right understanding of God. As we see in Ephesians 1:3–14, we are brought into a saving relationship with God through the sovereign election of the Father (vv. 3–6a), the redemptive work on the cross of Jesus Christ (vv. 6b–12), and the application of that work by the Spirit as a pledge to us of the hopeful future that is to come (vv. 13–14).

[29] But it is necessary for eternal salvation that one also believe in the incarnation of our Lord Jesus Christ faithfully. [30] Now this is the true faith: that we believe and confess that our Lord Jesus Christ, God's Son, is both God and man, equally. [31] He is God from the essence of the Father, begotten before time; [32] completely God, completely man, with a rational soul and human flesh; [33] equal to the Father as regards divinity, less than the Father as regards humanity.

The second main part of the creed restates and summarizes the Christology of both Nicaea and Chalcedon. Nothing new is offered, but orthodoxy is affirmed. The creed begins here by asserting the necessity of all Christians who desire 'eternal salvation' to 'believe in the incarnation of our Lord Jesus Christ faithfully.' As examined earlier, it is not the belief that Jesus is the Father's lesser servant who brings about redemption (contra Arius), but rather that the Lord Jesus Christ is truly God in human flesh who came down from heaven to save His people.

What is the core of 'true faith'? It is 'that we believe and confess that our Lord Jesus Christ,' who we know is 'God's son, is both God and man, equally.' This statement brings us back into thinking about and affirming the hypostatic union of Jesus Christ. Both natures of Christ—'completely God, completely man'—are represented here. As God, the creed reaffirms that the Son is Himself 'God from the essence of the Father, begotten before time.' He is of the same essence, or substance, as the Father, and thereby truly divine in every way. As to His relation to the Father, the Son is 'begotten before time' (eternally generated) and 'equal to the Father as regards divinity.'

The creed also affirms the true humanity of Jesus Christ, 'completely man, with a rational soul and human flesh.' This statement (reminiscent of the language in the Definition of Chalcedon) opposes the erroneous beliefs of Apollinarianism—that Christ was not fully human in

His incarnation. Here the creed doubles down on the full humanity of Jesus. Yet while the Son is consubstantial and coequal with the Father eternally, in the incarnation He is 'less than the Father as regards humanity.' In this way the incarnate Son is subordinate to the Father in his humanity (Luke 22:42; John 6:38; etc.).

[34] Although he is God and man, yet Christ is not two, but one. [35] He is one, however, not by his divinity being turned into flesh, but by God's taking humanity to himself. [36] He is one, certainly not by the blending of his essence, but by the unity of his person. [37] For just as one man is both rational soul and flesh, so too the one Christ is both God and man.

After affirming the actuality of the hypostatic union of Jesus Christ, the creed rehearses the known particulars of this union. How does the union of the two natures of Christ exist? Nestorianism and Monophysitism attempted to explain this reality, but utterly failed to do so. And while the creed does not solve the mystery, it gives us orthodox language for how we are to understand it.

The doctrine of the hypostatic union of Jesus Christ is that He is one person with two natures—God and man. Line 35 expresses that this union ('He is one') is not accomplished 'by his divinity being turned into flesh.' He does not lose or surrender any aspect of His deity. Rather, as Philippians 2:7 affirms, this occurs 'by God's taking humanity to himself.' Understood correctly, the eternal Son takes on humanity in his incarnation.

In opposition to the Monophysite heresy—that Christ's two natures blended together to form one new nature—the creed maintains, 'He is one, certainly not by the blending of his essence, but by the unity of his person.' Line 37 consists of what scholars refer to as the *Soul-Flesh* analogy. In trying to understand how the two natures of Christ were united, Cyril of Alexandria popularized the analogy of the convergence of the human soul and body.[13] In the same way that a human being is not divided in their soul and body, but perfectly and unnoticeably united, so it is with the divine and human natures of Christ. Following this reasoning, the creed asserts: 'For just as one man is both rational soul and flesh, so too the one Christ is both God and man.' The whole purpose of lines 34 through 37 is to express unequivocally the perfect union of the two natures of Jesus Christ.

[38] He suffered for our salvation; he descended to hell; he arose from the dead on the third day; [39] he ascended to heaven; he is seated at the Father's right hand; [40] from there he will come to judge the living and the dead. [41] At his coming all people will arise bodily [42] and give an accounting of their own deeds. [43] Those who have done good will enter eternal life, and those who have done evil will enter eternal fire.

Lines 38 and 39 are very similar to those of the Nicene Creed. They articulate the saving work of Christ on the cross. 'He suffered for our salvation' no doubt includes his suffering under Pontius Pilate, bloody crucifixion, and agonizing death. Like with the later versions of the Apostles' Creed, this creed expresses the sentiment that 'he descended to hell'—a statement of Christ's own descent into the grave, not as a theological belief that He physically went to hell. The vindication of his saving work came as 'he arose from the dead on the third day; he ascended to heaven; he is seated at the Father's right hand.' Line 40 articulates the second coming of Christ to earth in

---

13. For an overview of the Soul-Flesh analogy, see J.N.D. Kelly, *The Athanasian Creed* (New York: Harper & Row, 1964), 98–104. For his comments and evaluation of Cyril of Alexandria's use of the analogy, see J.N.D. Kelly, *Early Christian Doctrines*. Revised Edition (New York: HarperOne, 1978), 321.

power and judgment: 'from there he will come to judge the living and the dead.'

Lines 41 through 43 articulate the future judgment taught in Revelation 20 whereby 'all people will arise bodily and give an accounting of their own deeds'—the saints resurrected to reign with Christ (Rev. 20:4, 6) while unrepentant sinners are judged (vv. 11–15). While it is to be understood that believers are saved through faith in Jesus Christ, the evidence of that faith comes in their deeds. The creed reflects such a distinction, noting: 'Those who have done good will enter eternal life, and those who have done evil will enter eternal fire' (cf. Rev. 20:12; Matt. 16:27; Rev. 2:23).

[44] This is the catholic faith: that one cannot be saved without believing it firmly and faithfully.
The closing line functions the same way the opening two lines do—to provide a serious warning to those who would play fast and loose with their faith. As referenced earlier, 'the catholic faith' is that which is affirmed as essential truth by the universal Christian church. However, our modern Protestant ears may be prone to ring and our guard goes up at the notion that 'one cannot be saved without believing [the catholic faith] firmly and faithfully.' After all, is not salvation by faith alone in Christ? It most certainly is (John 14:6; Rom. 3:28; Gal. 2:16).

Yet salvation embodies more than just our acknowledgment of gospel facts. True salvation—God's regenerating a spiritually dead person and adopting them as redeemed children (cf. Rom. 8:14–17; Col. 1:13–14)—bears itself out in the transformation of the believer's whole life, which includes their understanding of the Triune God. And while it is possible, as Donald Fairbairn discusses, that the Athanasian Creed leans too far toward the doctrine of the Middle Ages which insists on works being added to faith,[14] we must not forget the argument from James 2:17–18: 'So also faith by itself, if it does not have works, is dead. But someone will say, "You have faith and I have works." Show me your faith apart from your works, and I will show you my faith by my works.' Sound faith must always result in right living. This includes 'firmly and faithfully' adhering to the body of sound Christian doctrine.

---

14. Fairbairn and Reeves, *The Story of Creeds and Confessions*, 137.

6

The Testimony of the
Protestant Confessions

The whole world changed drastically in the thousand years between the Council of Chalcedon and the Protestant Reformation. The Western Roman Empire fell at the end of the fifth century due to the barbarian invasions which eventually resulted in the advent of the Middle Ages (also known as the Medieval Period). It was during this period of time that the churches in the East (Orthodox) and West (Catholic) split in what came to be known as the Great Schism of 1054. However, the Roman Catholic Church continued in corruption as religious culture degraded. For centuries, the power structure in Rome had ballooned while the commoner was held captive through spiritual abuse, superstition, and mysticism. Through it all, however, Christ sustained the remnant of his true church.

While the tremors of Reformation were already rumbling in the years leading up to the sixteenth century, it was the German monk Martin Luther's fateful stance against Rome's abuses that ignited the firestorm known as Protestantism. When Luther nailed his *95 Theses* to the castle door at Wittenberg on October 31, 1517, he had only initially intended to address the problem of religious abuses. In the years that followed, however, it became apparent to Luther and others that many key components of Western Christianity needed to be reformed from the inside out.

In earlier centuries, church councils met together to identify individual errors that needed correcting. As we saw in the previous chapters, the result of the first four ecumenical councils was the creation of two short documents: the Nicene Creed and the Definition of Chalcedon. But these were targeted efforts to root out heresies; they were not blueprints to overhaul the whole religious system. By the time of the Protestant Reformation, the religious leaders throughout Europe began writing treatises and drafting doctrinal confessions in order to re-establish the bounds of biblical orthodoxy moving forward.

Whereas a *creed* is a short summary statement of essential doctrine, *confessions* offer an expanded view of theology applied to all aspects of religious life and practice. Over the course of the sixteenth and seventeenth centuries, numerous Protestant confessions were written and used by churches all throughout the Christian world. While these various confessions tackled a bevy of issues and spoke to many aspects of theology, the vast majority of them rearticulated and expounded on the essential doctrines ruled on by the early church. In this chapter we will look briefly at how several key confessions articulated the doctrines contained in the early church creeds—namely the full deity of the Son and the Spirit, and the doctrine of the Trinity.

THE AUGSBURG CONFESSION (1530)

Efforts toward Reformation were not initially well-received within the Holy Roman Empire. Martin Luther and his companions, along with other Reformers from other regions such as France and Switzerland, came to be regarded as enemies of the Church of Rome. In addition, there was much infighting between many of the Protestant leaders, most famously between Luther and Ulrich Zwingli over the issue of the Lord's Supper. The rift would never be mended.

In the midst of turmoil, however, several political leaders, such as Philip of Hesse, sought to vindicate the cause of the Reformation in Germany. In order to be seen as more than just an erratic religious movement, Luther and his allies would have to present a legitimate statement and arguments for consideration. While Luther and his colleague Philip Melanchthon had written several statements of faith—as well as the first Protestant catechisms in 1529—a more definitive statement was needed. Philip of Hesse and others successfully lobbied Emperor Charles V to hear the new Lutheran statement at the imperial diet held in Augsburg in 1530.

While the backbone of the new confession consisted of the labors of both Luther and Melanchthon, it was ultimately Melanchthon who penned the final draft to be submitted at Augsburg. While it did not ultimately win over the emperor to the Protestant cause, the Augsburg Confession succeeded in legitimizing the efforts of the early Reformers. The Augsburg Confession was eventually adopted into the Lutheran Book of Concord (1580) along with eight other documents, which included the Apostles' Creed, the Nicene Creed, and the Athanasian Creed.

While the confession tackles numerous doctrinal points in twenty-eight articles, the first twenty-one follow the contour of the Apostles' Creed. In the first article, the confession articulates the orthodox view of God as expressed also in the Nicene Creed:

[1] Our churches, with common consent, do teach that the decree of the Council of Nicaea concerning the Unity of the

Divine Essence and concerning the Three Persons, [2] is true and to be believed without any doubting; that is to say, there is one Divine Essence which is called and which is God: eternal, without body, without parts, of infinite power, wisdom, and goodness, the Maker and Preserver of all things, visible and invisible; [3] and yet there are three Persons, of the same essence and power, who also are coeternal, the Father, the Son, and the Holy Ghost. [4] And the term 'person' they use as the Fathers have used it, to signify, not a part or quality in another, but that which subsists of itself (Article 1:1–4).[1]

In a brilliantly concise paragraph, the first four lines of the opening article summarize and confess the essential elements of all the early creeds. It confesses the 'unity' and oneness of the divine essence, as well as articulates the belief in the three persons of the Godhead as expressed in the Athanasian Creed.

Article 3 of the confession deals with the doctrine of the Son of God. While much of the language of the article is near verbatim to the Apostles' Creed, it also weaves in elements from the Definition of Chalcedon, even elaborating further. It maintains that the Son is 'two natures, the divine and the human, inseparably enjoined in one Person, one Christ, true God and true man'—a beautiful summation of Chalcedonian Christology. Beyond this, there are gospel elements woven in, as Christ is said to 'reconcile the Father unto us, and be a sacrifice, not only for original guilt, but also for all actual sins of men.' The confession extols in not only a divine Christ, but a saving Christ who restores His people back to the Father through His own sacrifice.

THE BELGIC CONFESSION (1561)

What we now know as the Belgic Confession was written by a French pastor named Guido de Brès, a student of the

---

1. Chad Van Dixhoorn, ed., *Creeds, Confessions, and Catechisms: A Reader's Edition* (Wheaton: Crossway, 2022), 35.

famed Genevan Reformer John Calvin. During the sixteenth century there was great persecution against the Reformed churches of Belgium and the Netherlands. As a way to plead for tolerance, de Brès penned the confession in 1561, modeled after the Gallic Confession of Calvin's design, in order to convince King Philip II of Spain—whose forces occupied the Low Countries—to show restraint. The purpose of the Belgic Confession was to demonstrate that the adherents to Reformation doctrine were not heretics or rebels but earnest Christians who were faithful to the Lord Jesus Christ.

Consisting of thirty-seven articles, the confession traverses a wide range of doctrine, with a heavy focus on traditional orthodoxy. Articles 8 through 11 consist of a robust treatment of the doctrine of the Trinity and the deity of Christ and the Holy Spirit.

Article 8 gives a lengthy statement on the Trinity, followed by a bevy of scriptural examples in Article 9. On the Trinity, the confession declares, 'we believe in one God, who is one single essence, in whom there are three persons, really, truly, and eternally distinct according to their incommunicable properties—namely, Father, Son, and Holy Spirit.' In addition to articulating the accepted mystery of orthodoxy, the confession makes reference to the 'distinct...incommunicable properties...[of] Father, Son, and Holy Spirit.' This is what we understand to be *modes of subsistence* or *eternal relations of origin*. The remainder of Article 8 reads much like the Athanasian Creed with regards to the explanation of the relations of the members of the Trinity. At the end of Article 9, the confession affirms:

> This doctrine of the Holy Trinity has always been maintained in the true church, from the time of the apostles until the present... And so, in this matter we willingly accept the three ecumenical creeds—the Apostles', Nicene, and Athanasian—

as well as what the ancient fathers decided in agreement with them.

On the deity of the Son, Article 10 weaves in creedal language, Scripture references, and logical arguments. It affirms Jesus Christ to be 'the only Son of God—eternally begotten, not made nor created, for then he would be a creature.' This speaks of Christ's eternal generation, by which the following affirmation is made: 'He is one in essence with the Father; coeternal; the exact image of the person of the Father and the "reflection of his glory," being in all things like him.' It is from this point that the bulk of the article builds, discussing the eternality of Christ, citing Hebrews 1:3, John 1:3, Colossians 1:16, and Hebrews 7:3. The driving force of the article is arrived at the conclusion: 'So then, he [Jesus Christ] is the true eternal God, the Almighty, whom we invoke, worship, and serve.' Beyond mere doctrinal statements of orthodoxy, the confession pledges earnest faithfulness to the Lord Jesus Christ.

Article 11 on the Spirit is briefer than the preceding articles in the section, but no less robust. Whereas the previous article confesses that Christ is 'eternally begotten' of the Father, the Spirit is affirmed to 'proceed eternally from the Father and the Son—neither made, nor created, nor begotten, but only proceeding from the two of them'—following the *Filioque* clause of the Athanasian Creed. The confession then affirms the full deity of the Holy Spirit as the third person of the Trinity, 'of one and the same essence, and majesty, and glory, with the Father and the Son.' Ever concerned to present the content of the confession as submissive to the Word of God, the final line pertaining to the Spirit declares: 'He is true and eternal God, as the Holy Scriptures teach us.'

THE HEIDELBERG CATECHISM (1563)

One of the most beloved Protestant catechisms of the last five centuries is the Heidelberg Catechism. While not a confession, it is a true *catechism*—a doctrinal statement framed in the form of questions and answers. The catechism was composed by Zacharias Ursinus, a professor of theology at Heidelberg University, with the help of Caspar Olevianus, at the request of Elector Frederick III of the Palatinate, a German province. The initial document was approved by the Heidelberg synod in January 1563, with other editions released in later years.

Consisting of 129 questions and answers, the catechism is divided into three main parts, patterned after the structure of Paul's letter to the Romans.[2] The 129 questions are broken down into fifty-two 'Lord's Day' readings, enough theological material to cover a year's worth of sermons. The Heidelberg Catechism opens with the timeless question for the ages: 'What is your only comfort in life and in death?' The answer is given: 'That I am not my own, but belong—body and soul, in life and in death—to my faithful Savior, Jesus Christ.'

While the doctrines expounded in the catechism are dripping with Scripture, it also makes fair use of the early church creeds. In fact, several of the questions and answers are short expositions of various lines of the Apostles' Creed.[3] However, the doctrinal expressions of the Trinity and the Son of God are reminiscent of the language of the Nicene, Chalcedonian, and Athanasian creeds.

The catechism's teaching on the doctrine of the Trinity is relatively brief but no less orthodox. Only two questions and answers address the doctrine explicitly (24 and 25). Question 24 asks about the thematic division of the Apostles' Creed quoted in Answer 23, to which the response is given: 'Into three

---

2. Joel R. Beeke and Sinclair B. Ferguson, eds., *Reformed Confessions Harmonized* (Grand Rapids: Baker Books, 1999), x.

3. Questions 22, 23, 26, 33–35, 37–39, 41, 44, 46, 50, 52–58.

parts: God the Father and our creation; God the Son and our deliverance; and God the Holy Spirit and our sanctification.' This expression gives voice to the coequality of the three members of the Trinity as God. The following question asks: 'Since there is only one divine being, why do you speak of three: Father, Son, and Holy Spirit?' Without rehashing all the arguments or creedal language, the catechism simply replies, 'Because that is how God has revealed himself in his Word: these three distinct persons are one, true, eternal God.'[4]

The catechism's teaching on the doctrine of the Son is more expansive. More than simply rehearsing creedal statements, the catechism reasons within itself, taking the Nicene and Chalcedon doctrine even further in rational thought. It presumes the *hypostatic union*—the uniting of the Son's divine and human natures—and poses the hypothetical question: 'Why must the mediator [Jesus Christ] be a true and righteous man?' to which the answer is given: 'Because God's justice requires that human nature, which has sinned, must pay for its sin; but a sinner could never pay for others' (Q/A 16). The inverse question is then asked: 'Why must he also be true God?' to which the reply comes: 'So that, by the power of his divinity, he might bear in his humanity the weight of God's wrath, and earn for us and restore to us righteousness and life' (Q/A 17). Again, the catechism pushes beyond the creeds and into the reasons for the truth.

On the nature of Christ, Q/A 33 succinctly explains the notion of Jesus Christ being God's 'only begotten Son' yet asks why we are also referred to as 'God's children.' The answer comes: 'Because Christ alone is the eternal, natural Son of God'— referring to the eternal generation of the Son explained in the

---

4. As proof of this statement, the catechism lists the following Scriptures: Matt. 3:16–17; 28:18–19; Luke 4:18 (Isa. 61:1); John 14:26; 15:26; 2 Cor. 13:14; Gal. 4:6; Titus 3:5–6.

Nicene and Chalcedon statements—'We, however, are adopted children of God—adopted by grace for the sake of Christ.' Not to delve too far into theological verbiage, Q/A 35 explains the reason for the incarnation, delving into the mystery of the joining of the two natures of Christ:

> That the eternal Son of God, who is and remains true and eternal God, took to himself, through the working of the Holy Spirit, from the flesh and blood of the virgin Mary, a true human nature so that he might also become David's true descendant, like his brothers in all things except sin.

In a further affirmation of both orthodoxy and comfort, Answer 47 articulates that 'Christ is true man and true God. In his human nature Christ is not now on earth; but in his divinity, majesty, grace, and Spirit he is never absent from us.' In statements such as this, the Heidelberg Catechism proves that not only is theology practical but also serves to comfort and encourage the true believer.

THE SECOND HELVETIC CONFESSION (1566)

The First Helvetic Confession was written in 1536 to function as teaching statement for the early Reformation among the Swiss people (*Helvetti* is the Latin term for the inhabitants of what is now Switzerland).[5] The First Confession found limited acceptance, but it was the Second Helvetic Confession that had the bigger impact. After being commissioned by Frederick III, Swiss pastor Heinrich Bullinger undertook to write an exposition of Reformation doctrine, which he completed in 1564. After some minor revisions, it was accepted at the Zurich conference in 1566.

---

5.   Beeke and Ferguson, *Reformed Confessions Harmonized*, x.

The confession consists of twenty thousand words over thirty chapters and was written with John Calvin's *Institutes of the Christian Religion* in mind, as well as the Counter-Reformation of the Council of Trent (1545–1563).[6] It is perhaps the most definitive doctrinal statement of early Reformed theology and was widely accepted by a large number of Reformed churches throughout Europe by the end of the sixteenth century. While the confession draws from Calvin's influence, Bullinger no doubt kept the early church creeds in clear view as he expounded on the doctrines expressed in the Word of God.

While not expansive, the confession articulates a view of the Trinity that aligns with the early creeds. It states: 'We…believe and teach that the same infinite, one, and indivisible God is in person inseparably and without confusion distinguished into the Father, the Son, and the Holy Spirit.' In defense of the hypothetical accusation of Tritheism, the confession explains:

> So that there are not three Gods, but three persons, consubstantial, coeternal, and coequal; distinct, as touching their persons; and, in order, one going before another, yet without any inequality. For, as touching their nature or essence, they are so joined together that they are but one God; and the divine essence is common to the Father, the Son, and the Holy Spirit (III:3).

Without naming its sources, the confession employs the use of the terms 'essence,' 'person,' and 'consubstantial'—no doubt derived from Nicene orthodoxy.

On the person of Jesus Christ, the confession affirms His full divinity and hypostatic union. In Chalcedonian style we read:

---

6.   Beeke and Ferguson, *Reformed Confessions Harmonized*, x.

> We acknowledge...that there be in one and the same Jesus
> Christ our Lord two natures—the divine and the human
> nature; and we say that these two are so conjoined or united
> that they are not swallowed up, confounded, or mingled
> together; but rather united or joined together in one person
> (the properties of each nature being safe and remaining still),
> so that we do worship one Christ our Lord, and not two (XI:6).

While the language is clearly creedal orthodoxy, the confession
even goes so far as to name the early opponents to sound
Christology. We read that 'our Lord Jesus Christ had not a
soul without sense and reason, as Apollinaris thought' (XI:5),
and 'we detest the heresy of Nestorius, which makes two
Christs of one and dissolves the union of each person, so do we
abominate the madness of Eutyches and of the Monothelites
and Monophysites, who overthrow the propriety of the human
nature' (XI:7). With the use of such phrases as 'we detest' and
'we abominate,' the confession's author, Heinrich Bullinger,
exudes the passion and conviction of the bishops who
contended earnestly for orthodoxy at early church councils.

THE WESTMINSTER CONFESSION OF FAITH (1647)

By the middle of the seventeenth century, the Reformation
had taken root in England, despite frequent opposition from
various kings and queens. However, the Puritan movement
soon sprouted up to further reform and purify the religious
practices that had gone awry within the Church of England.
When King Charles I was deposed in 1642, the Puritan
Parliament took over control of England.

One of the first proactive measures carried out by Parliament
was the convening of the Westminster Assembly from 1643 to
1653. The main goal of the assembly was to develop specific
theological and ecclesiastical measures to aid in carrying out
the full reform of the Church of England. Of the many tasks the

assembly accomplished was the production of a Shorter and Longer Catechism, as well as a hearty confession of faith. In the end, 121 theologians, along with thirty laymen and Scottish advisors, produced what R.C. Sproul calls 'the most precise and accurate summary of the content of biblical Christianity ever set forth in a creedal form.'[7]

While much of the content reflects the Reformed efforts of previous confessions (such as the Helvetic Confessions, the Formula of Concord, and the Irish Articles),[8] it also reflects the work of John Calvin and others. However, on the matters of theology proper and Christology, the confession draws inspiration from the early church creeds.

In the confession's discussion of the doctrine of the Trinity, it states:

> In the unity of the Godhead there be three persons, of one substance, power, and eternity: God the Father, God the Son, and God the Holy Ghost: the Father is of none, neither begotten, nor proceeding; the Son is eternally begotten of the Father; the Holy Ghost eternally proceeding from the Father and the Son (II:3).

Not only does the Trinitarian formula appear from the era of the Athanasian Creed, the reference to the oneness of the divine 'substance' is from the days of Nicaea. Each member of the Trinity is labeled as 'God,' thus further emphasizing their divine coequality. There is also the clear expression of the eternal relations of the members—the Father's *paternity* (not 'begotten, nor proceeding'), the Son's *filiation* ('eternally begotten of the Father'), and the double procession of the Spirit's *spiration* ('eternally proceeding from the Father and the Son').

---

7. R.C. Sproul, *Truths We Confess: A Systematic Exposition of the Westminster Confession of Faith* (Sanford: Reformation Trust, 2019), 1.

8. Beeke and Ferguson, *Reformed Confessions Harmonized*, xii.

While any specific discussion of the divinity of the Holy Spirit is absent from the confession (inherent in the discussion of the Trinity), it expounds generously on the nature and offices of Christ. Reflecting the language of Nicaea and Chalcedon, the confession refers to Christ as 'The Son of God, the second person in the Trinity...very and eternal God, of one substance and equal with the Father.' Regarding the two natures of Christ, the confession cites the virgin birth as the culmination of this union, 'so that two whole, perfect, and distinct natures, the Godhead and the manhood, were inseparably joined together in one person, without conversion, composition, or confusion. Which person is very God, and very man, yet one Christ, the only Mediator between God and man (VIII:2).'

However, the recitation of orthodox Christology is not simply for its own sake. The confession reasons that 'Christ, in the work of mediation, acts according to both natures, by each nature doing that which is proper to itself' (VIII:7). In other words, the fact that Christ functions as our divine mediator, securing salvation for us, is directly connected to His identity as the God-man. In this way, understanding the glorious mystery of the incarnation of the Son is not simply an intellectual and theological exercise. Rather we are meant to ponder the glorious splendor of Christ and praise Him for who He is and what He has done for us.

THE LONDON BAPTIST CONFESSION OF FAITH (1689)

The London Baptist Confession of Faith has become the standard Reformed Baptist confession. It finds its origination in 1644 (revised in 1646) when the Particular Baptists were persecuted in England. However, in attempt to distance themselves from heretical groups of 'Anabaptists,' the confession was revised in 1677 (and later published in 1689) in order to demonstrate further unity with the Presbyterians and Congregationalists.[9] Adapted from the Westminster Confession of Faith (1647) and the Savoy Declaration (1658), the confession seeks to expound Reformed doctrine yet offers significant modification of previous statements with regard to the doctrine of the church and the sacraments, especially baptism.

Having drawn from a deep confessional well, much of the content reflects Reformed orthodoxy from previous years. Yet we see the same precision when articulating the issues addressed by the early church. On the doctrine of the Trinity, the third paragraph of chapter 2 combines various statements from the First London Baptist Confession, the Westminster Confession, and the Savoy Declaration and, as Samuel Waldron notes, 'thus provides a more detailed statement of the Trinity than any of them.'[10] It expresses the following regarding the Godhead:

> In this divine and infinite Being there are three subsistences, the Father, the Word (or Son), and Holy Spirit, of one substance, power, and Eternity, each having the whole Divine Essence, yet the Essence undivided, the Father is of none neither begotten nor proceeding, the Son is Eternally begotten of the Father, the holy Spirit proceeding from the Father and the Son, all infinite, without beginning, therefore but one God, who is not to be divided in nature and Being; but distinguished by several peculiar, relative properties, and personal relations; which doctrine of the Trinity is the foundation of all our Communion with God, and comfortable dependence on him.

---

9. I am indebted to D. Scott Meadows for this observation.

10. Samuel E. Waldron, *A Modern Exposition of the 1689 Baptist Confession of Faith* (Faverdale North: Evangelical Press, 1989), 55–56.

The phrase, 'the whole Divine Essence, yet the Essence undivided,' is beautifully unique to this confession. The rehearsal of creedal orthodoxy is clear and pronounced, followed by an insightful note, that the 'doctrine of the Trinity is the foundation of all our Communion with God, and comfortable dependence on him.' More than cold, theological words on a page, the expressions of the Godhead inspire in us faith, hope, love, and obedience—a true communion with God.

Chapter 8 of the confession expounds the doctrine of Christ in similar terms as the Westminster Confession. It affirms him to be 'the second Person in the Holy Trinity, being very and eternal God.' Reflecting Nicene orthodoxy, the Son is stated to be 'of one substance and equal with him [the Father]' and was 'conceived by the Holy Spirit in the Womb of the Virgin Mary.' This perfect union of Christ's two natures are 'inseparably joined together in one Person: without conversion, composition, or confusion,' as is true to Chalcedonian Christology.

CONCLUSION

In the final analysis we see that every major Protestant denomination (Lutheran, Anglican, Presbyterian, Baptist, etc.) that identifies with its confessional heritage also relies on the doctrinal work done by the early church through the writing of the creeds. And while modern sensibilities tend to spurn the things that are deemed to be 'old' there can be no escaping the truth that the early church creeds lay the foundation of essential orthodoxy, of which the cornerstone is none other than the Word of God.

7

The Creeds for Today

As we have seen, the early church creeds have proven to be faithful statements of biblical doctrine and have been widely accepted by the universal church for centuries. By the time of the Protestant Reformation, key leaders like Martin Luther, Heinrich Bullinger, and Caspar Olevianus were drawing heavily from the creeds. Even John Calvin patterned his magnum opus, *Institutes of the Christian Religion*, after the structure of the Apostles' Creed. Post-Reformation scholar Francis Turretin wrote that while creeds 'do not have the same authority as the Scriptures...they have even their own memorable weight and ought to be valued very highly by the pious.'[1] In more recent times, Christian leaders like Charles H. Spurgeon, B.B. Warfield, J.I. Packer, and R.C. Sproul have expressed their ardent appreciation for the creeds. So, why are they seemingly absent from the modern Christian landscape?

As I have hinted throughout this book, I tend to think that there are several aversions to the ancient creeds—one being the fear of embracing creeds at the expense of Scripture; another is the false notion that anything 'old' is not valuable for today.

---

1. Francis Turretin, *Institutes of Elenctic Theology*. George Musgrave Giger, trans., James T. Dennison, Jr., ed. (Phillipsburg: P&R Publishing, 1992), 3:282–283.

But even our cursory study thus far has revealed that there is so much for us to gain in understanding the doctrines contained in the early creeds. And as we look to appropriate what we have learned, let us focus in on a few areas where we can defend the truths of Christianity and continue to grow in our faith.

MAGNIFYING CHRIST

We are living in a cultural moment where there are so many churches that talk incessantly about Jesus Christ yet seem to say very little about him. Furthermore, it seems, on the surface at least, that the general professing Christian population knows even less about *who* he is or *what* he has done. The tendency is often either to diminish the Lord, bringing him down to our level, or to assign words and actions to him that are out of line with his character. But as believers we ought to oppose any and all falsehoods about Christ, and that's where the creeds can prove helpful to us.

Of course, the primary opposition to sound belief about Jesus Christ tends to come from other religions and cults. Islam, for example, teaches that there is one true God, but does not regard Jesus as God Himself or the Son of God. He is seen as one of many prophets of Islam, in the line before their greatest prophet, Muhammad. And while it does acknowledge Jesus' virgin birth, personal piety, and miraculous ministry, Islam does not see Jesus as anything more than a man.[2]

In a similar vein, both Mormonism (known as the Church of Jesus Christ of Latter-day Saints) and the Jehovah's Witnesses (known as the Watchtower Society)[3] teach that Jesus is a created being and regarded to be God's 'only-begotten Son' in

---

2. One of the more helpful Protestant evaluations of Islam is James R. White, *What Every Christian Needs to Know about the Qur'an* (Minneapolis: Bethany House Publishers, 2013).

3. For an evaluation of both of these groups, see Walter Martin, *The Kingdom of the Cults* (Minneapolis: Bethany House Publishers, 1985.)

a physical, temporal sense. The LDS Church teaches that Jesus is a human man who *became* a god, which models how other humans can do the same. The Watchtower Society teaches that Jesus was merely the archangel Michael who came to earth as a man and who was later assumed back into heaven after his earthly death.

In each of the instances listed above, Jesus Christ is diminished and devalued. He is not affirmed or esteemed in keeping with Scripture—as Lord, Savior, Word, or God. Yet the complete witness of Scripture is synthesized in the simple creedal statements that Jesus Christ is 'God of God, Light of Light, very God of very God; begotten, not made, being of one substance with the Father, by whom all things were made' (the Nicene Creed). Furthermore, the Definition of Chalcedon declares that:

> our Lord Jesus Christ [is] the same perfect in divinity and perfect in humanity, the same truly God and truly man… begotten before the ages from the Father as regards his divinity, and in the last days the same for us and for our salvation from Mary, the virgin God-bearer, as regards his humanity; one and the same Christ, Son, Lord, only-begotten, acknowledged in two natures…

In a day when there is already so much ignorance about the person of Jesus Christ, no doubt fueled by confusion perpetuated by false religions, we need a revival of orthodox, biblical Christology that can give language to what is true about our Lord. Rehearsing creedal language about Christ does not bring Him down low or nullify Scripture's power or authority. Rather the early creeds affirm and echo the faithful and true testimony that Jesus Christ is to be magnified, adored, and worshiped as Almighty God in human flesh.

UNDERSTANDING THE HOLY SPIRIT

One of the most abused doctrines in Christianity is that of the Holy Spirit. Some of the issues have to do with understanding the Spirit's ministry—how He works and what ought to be attributed to Him. However, a greater problem is the misunderstanding of the Holy Spirit as a *person*, even as a *divine* person.

So often, well-intended Christians act as though the Holy Spirit is an 'it' and not a *He*. They treat Him as though He were merely a powerful force, or a mystical energy that flows in and out of their lives by chance. They might even try to channel His power and wield Him like a spiritual tool that can be used to serve their own desires. But this is terrible error.

In many places in Scripture we see the Spirit function as a person. For example, He exercises a mind full of deep understanding (1 Cor. 2:10), He makes decisions (1 Cor. 12:7–11), and He can be grieved (Eph. 4:30). More than this, He functions as a divine person—as God. The apostles treat the Spirit as God in Acts 5:3–4. He is sent in the place of Jesus Christ to minister as God (John 14:16, 26; 16:13). Furthermore, He is regarded as equal to the Father and Son (e.g. Matt. 3:16; 28:19; 2 Cor. 13:14; Eph. 2:18; 4:4–6; 1 Pet. 1:2).

The early creeds affirm Scripture's teaching and attribute all of the fullness of deity to the third person of the Trinity. As we saw, church leaders like Athanasius and the Cappadocian fathers wrote extensively on the Spirit's deity, arguing for His rightful place within the divine triad. While the Apostles' Creed does nothing more than acknowledge the Holy Spirit, the Nicene Creed confesses the Spirit as 'the Lord and Giver of life'—hardly an *it* but rather a divine person; 'who proceeds from the Father and the Son'—an affirmation of the eternal relationship with the other members of the Trinity. Furthermore, we understand that the Spirit is to be 'worshiped and glorified' along with the Father and Son, which is only appropriate if He is fully and completely God.

The Athanasian Creed fills out the doctrine of the Holy Spirit by identifying His place within the Trinity. Line 5 notes that the Spirit is a 'distinct person,' yet the divinity of the three is shared (line 6). Along with the Father and Son, His glory is equal and His majesty coeternal; He is also uncreated, immeasurable, and eternal (lines 8 through 10); He is Almighty (line 13). Line 15 states clearly: 'The Holy Spirit is God.' Not only does this doctrinal rehearsal affirm the unity of the Trinity, but for the sake of the Holy Spirit's personhood, it rightly affirms the key aspects of who He is and why He is to be worshiped as God.

EMBRACING THE TRINITY

For those who embrace the doctrine of the Trinity, it almost seems odd that, after more than sixteen hundred years of settled orthodoxy, there would be a person claiming to be a Christian who would deny the Trinity. Yet there are scores of professing believers who deny the Trinity, either convictionally or functionally.

Ministering in New England, I am intimately acquainted with the damage done to all the Congregational churches in the mid-1800s. Unitarianism wreaked havoc by displacing the Reformed Trinitarian theology of the American Puritans and Great Awakeners. Early Unitarians rejected the Nicene Creed's assertion that God is one being existing in three *hypostases*— Father, Son, and Spirit. They believed that by rejecting this doctrine they were returning to a 'primitive' form of Christianity that was truer to its original founding. This book has gone to great lengths to argue that both the Bible and the witness of the historical church affirm Trinitarian theology. Of course, the proof is in the pudding; today, the Unitarian churches in the Northeast have corrupted themselves altogether and rejected every tenet of the gospel in favor of the liberalized theology of progressivism.

One of the more present and insidious affronts to orthodox Trinitarianism today is the prevalence of Oneness Pentecostalism. Emerging only in the last century, Oneness Pentecostalism (also known as the Jesus Only Movement) teaches the view that there is one God who manifests Himself in different modes at different times. This modern movement is essentially a dressed-up iteration of the Modalistic Monarchianism of the third century. However, this movement is continuing to grow in popularity, especially in charismatic circles. Yet it poses a substantial threat to knowing the true and living God, as we understand that our God is triune in nature—the Father, the Son, and the Spirit eternally existing as one God in three distinct persons.[4]

The early creeds reflect the historic church's understanding and affirmation of the Triune God of the Scriptures. Put succinctly by the Athanasian Creed: 'Thus, the Father is God, the Son is God, the Holy Spirit is God' (line 15). But this is more than simply an affirmation of orthodoxy. As Michael Reeves notes, 'To know the Trinity is to know God, an eternal and personal God of infinite beauty, interest and fascination.'[5] It is right thinking about the true and wonderful God. Far from being a dry, sterile doctrine, 'the triune being of God is the vital oxygen of Christian life and joy.'[6]

CONTENDING EARNESTLY

We should not think that rehearsing a series of ancient creeds will somehow protect us from every doctrinal error in the world.

---

4. For a helpful critique of Oneness Pentecostalism, see Michael R. Burgos Jr., *Against Oneness Pentecostalism: An Exegetical-Theological Critique* (Church Militant Publications, 2020).

5. Michael Reeves, *Delighting in the Trinity: An Introduction to the Christian Faith* (Downers Grove: IVP Academic, 2012), 12.

6. Reeves, *Delighting in the Trinity*, 18.

In fact, the only true armor we have is found in the Word of God (cf. Eph. 6:10–17). However, familiarizing ourselves with the core affirmations of our faith can be helpful to us as believers. It trains us to think systematically, formulating our confessions of the totality of Scripture into phrases that we can embrace. Knowing the creeds also builds confidence that we are standing on the shoulders of saints who have gone before us and contended earnestly for the faith.

Furthermore, creeds give us bold doctrinal statements that provide more clarity, not less. This is appealing in our modern religious context that seems bent on minimizing the core essentials until we reach an absolute lowest common denominator version of Christianity. As biblical literacy plummets and theological knowledge degrades, we need to reclaim robust declarations full of theological words and phrases—all derived from the Scriptures.

When we really examine the hard work and earnest seeking of the early church, we realize that their labors did not produce statements that work against the Bible. They explain the Bible because they are submitted to it. In the end, may we not walk away with this obstinate declaration: Christ *or* creed! Rather let us 'retain the standard of sound words,' as Scripture commands us, and posture ourselves in such a way that we can wholeheartedly confess the Word of Jesus Christ our Lord and also embrace the standards of orthodoxy given to us in the early church creeds.

Glossary

Apollinarianism: The heretical teaching that Jesus is truly divine but not truly human.

Arianism: The heretical teaching that Jesus is a created being, less than God, and not truly God Himself.

Begotten: Expresses the Son's eternal relation to the Father. Also known as *filiation*.

Catechism: A doctrinal statement framed in the form of questions and answers.

Catholic: A reference to the universal nature of the church.

Confession: An expanded statement of Christian doctrine.

Creed: From the Latin word *credo*, which means 'I believe,' a statement of personal faith or affirmation of essential Christian truth.

Eternal Generation: The understanding that the Son is eternally begotten from the essence of the Father.

Eutychianism: The heretical teaching that the two natures of the Son are merged or blended into one new nature. Also known as *Monophysitism*.

Filioque: A term that refers to the Spirit proceeding from both the Father and the Son.

Homoiousios: A term that refers to the belief in Jesus being of a similar substance as the Father.

Homoousios: ('consubstantial') A term that refers to the belief in Jesus being of the same substance as the Father.

Hypostasis: Refers to the personhood of God.

Hypostatic Union: The doctrine of the mysterious union of the two natures (divine and human) of the Son in one person.

Modalism: The heretical teaching that there is only one person of God who manifested Himself in different modes at different times. Also known as *Sabellianism*.

Modes of Subsistence: The way the individual members of the divine Trinity are eternally related to one another. Also known as *Eternal Relations of Origin*.

Nestorianism: The heretical teaching that Jesus was two distinct persons—one divine nature indwelling one distinct human body.

Ousios: Refers to the Being or essence of God.

Procession: Expresses the Spirit's eternal relation to the Father and the Son. Also known as *spiration*.

Repentance: A change of mind that agrees with God about sin and the need for forgiveness; or a turning away from sin in obedience to the commands of God.

Sanctification: The Spirit-empowered work in the soul of the believer to grow them in Christlikeness.

Trinity: The term used to express one God who exists eternally in three distinct persons: the Father, the Son, and the Holy Spirit.

Tritheism: The heretical teaching that there are three distinct gods, rather than one Triune God.

Recommended Reading

GENERAL

Donald Fairbairn and Ryan M. Reeves, *The Story of Creeds and Confessions: Tracing the Development of the Christian Faith.* Grand Rapids: Baker Academic, 2019.

Justin S. Holcomb, *Know the Creeds and Councils.* Grand Rapids: Zondervan, 2014.

Carl R. Trueman, *The Creedal Imperative.* Wheaton: Crossway, 2012.

Chad Van Dixhoorn, ed., *Creeds, Confessions, and Catechisms.* Wheaton: Crossway, 2022.

THE APOSTLES' CREED

Alister McGrath, *'I Believe': Exploring the Apostles' Creed.* Downers Grove: InterVarsity Press, 1997.

Caspar Olevianus, *An Exposition of the Apostles' Creed.* Grand Rapids: Reformation Heritage Books, 2009.

R.C. Sproul, *What We Believe: Understanding and Confessing the Apostles' Creed.* Grand Rapids: Baker Books, 2015.

Herman Witsius, *Sacred Dissertations on the Apostles' Creed.* Grand Rapids: Reformation Heritage Books, repr. 2010.

NICENE ORTHODOXY AND BEYOND

Lewis Ayres, *Nicaea and its Legacy: An Approach to Fourth-Century Trinitarian Theology*. Oxford: Oxford University Press, 2004.

Henry Chadwick, *The Early Church*. Revised Edition. New York: Penguin Books, 1993.

J.N.D. Kelly, *Early Christian Doctrines*. Revised Edition. New York: HarperOne, 1978.

Michael Reeves, *Delighting in the Trinity: An Introduction to the Christian Faith*. Downers Grove: IVP Academic, 2012.

PROTESTANT CONFESSIONS

Joel R. Beeke and Sinclair B. Ferguson, eds, *Reformed Confessions Harmonized*. Grand Rapids: Baker Books, 1999.

Kevin DeYoung, *The Good News We Almost Forgot: Rediscovering the Gospel in a 16th Century Catechism*. Chicago: Moody Publishers, 2010.

James M. Renihan, *For the Vindication of the Truth: A Brief Exposition of the First London Baptist Confession of Faith*. Cape Coral: Founders Press, 2021.

R.C. Sproul, *Truths We Confess: A Systematic Exposition of the Westminster Confession of Faith*. Revised Edition. Orlando: Reformation Trust, 2019.

Acknowledgements

It is important that I begin by expressing my thankfulness to the Lord Jesus Christ who permits me to write. It's a mercy that I even have a ministry at all (2 Cor. 4:1), and pure grace that that ministry includes the blessing of writing books. All praise and glory belong to Him.

My sincere thanks to Christian Focus for partnering with me in this project, especially Willie MacKenzie, Rosanna Burton, and Colin Fast, as well as the many others who have diligently worked behind the scenes to bring this book to print.

I'm deeply indebted to my friend Scott Meadows for carefully reading an early draft of this manuscript and providing necessary feedback. He patiently and graciously worked with me to fine-tune the doctrinal expression of the book. He deserves much credit. Additionally, I am very greatful to Dr. Michael Haykin for his keen theological insights that helped put a sharper edge on the content in several places. Any mistakes are solely mine.

Finally, I owe a debt of gratitude to my wife, Jessica, for encouraging me to continue writing. She is ever patient and kind to me, loving me with the selfless love of Christ. Additionally, my children are joyfully patient with me, frequently asking me about my projects, and rejoicing with me when they are completed. I love you all, my darlings.

Christian Focus Publications

Our mission statement –

STAYING FAITHFUL

In dependence upon God we seek to impact the world through literature faithful to His infallible Word, the Bible. Our aim is to ensure that the Lord Jesus Christ is presented as the only hope to obtain forgiveness of sin, live a useful life and look forward to heaven with Him.

Our books are published in four imprints:

CHRISTIAN FOCUS

Popular works including biographies, commentaries, basic doctrine and Christian living.

CHRISTIAN HERITAGE

Books representing some of the best material from the rich heritage of the church.

MENTOR

Books written at a level suitable for Bible College and seminary students, pastors, and other serious readers. The imprint includes commentaries, doctrinal studies, examination of current issues and church history.

CF4•K

Children's books for quality Bible teaching and for all age groups: Sunday school curriculum, puzzle and activity books; personal and family devotional titles, biographies and inspirational stories – because you are never too young to know Jesus!

Christian Focus Publications Ltd,
Geanies House, Fearn, Ross-shire,
IV20 1TW, Scotland, United Kingdom.
www.christianfocus.com